CATECHIST GUIDE

Believe Celebrate Live™

Eucharist

Preparing to Celebrate First Communion

The Subcommittee on the Catechism, United States Conference of Catholic Bishops, has found the doctrinal content of this manual, copyright 2017, to be in conformity with the *Catechism of the Catholic Church*.

Nihil Obstat
Rev. Matthew S. Ernest, S.T.D.
Rev. Kevin J. O'Reilly, S.T.D.
Censores Librorum

Imprimatur
✠ His Eminence,
Timothy Cardinal Dolan
Archbishop of New York
May 12, 2017

The *Nihil Obstat* and *Imprimatur* are official declarations that a book or pamphlet is free of doctrinal or moral error. No implication is contained therein that those who have granted the *Nihil Obstat* and *Imprimatur* agree with the contents, opinions, or statements expressed.

Believe • Celebrate • Live™
... developed by the community of faith through...

Catechetical and Liturgical Consultants
Carole M. Eipers, D.Min.
National Catechetical Advisor
William H. Sadlier, Inc.

Donna Eschenauer, Ph.D.
Associate Dean
St. Joseph's Seminary
Yonkers, NY

Matthew Halbach, Ph.D.
Director
St. Joseph Education Center
Des Moines, IA

Tom Kendzia, B.Mus.Ed.
Composer and Director of Music
Christ the King Parish
Kingston, RI

Barbara Sutton, D.Min.
Associate Dean of Ministerial Formation and Outreach
St. John's School of Theology and Seminary
Collegeville, MN

Theological Consultants
Most Reverend Edward K. Braxton, Ph.D., S.T.D.
Official Theological Consultant
Bishop of Belleville

Monsignor John E. Pollard, S.T.L.
Pastor, Queen of All Saints Basilica
Chicago, IL

Reverend Donald Senior, CP, Ph.D., S.T.D.
Member, Pontifical Biblical Commission
President Emeritus of Catholic Theological Union
Chicago, IL

Inculturation Consultants
C. Vanessa White, Ph.D.
Catholic Theological Union
Chicago, IL

Dulce M. Jiménez-Abreu
Director of Bilingual Religion Markets
William H. Sadlier, Inc.

Luis J. Medina, M.A.
Bilingual Consultant
St. Louis, MO

Curriculum and Child Development Consultant
Thomas S. Quinlan, M.Div.
Director, Religious Education Office
Diocese of Joliet

Special Needs Consultants
Charleen Katra, M.A.
Associate Director Specializing in Disability Ministry
Archdiocese of Galveston-Houston

Madonna Wojtaszek-Healy, Ph.D.
Consultant for Special Needs, Religious Education Office
Diocese of Joliet

Media/Technology Consultant
Spirit Juice Studios
Chicago, IL

Sadlier Consulting Team
Suzan Larroquette
Director of Catechetical Consultant Services

Kathy Hendricks
National Catechetical Consultant

Timothy R. Regan
Regional Vice President

Writing/Development Team
Diane Lampitt, M.Ed.
Vice President, Product Management, Religion

Alexandra Rivas-Smith
Executive Vice President, Product Management

Mary Carol Kendzia
Research and Development Director, Religion

Joanne McDonald
Editorial Director

Regina Kelly
Supervising Editor

William M. Ippolito
Director of Corporate Planning

Editors
Ellen Marconi, Dignory Reina, Gloria Shahin, Robert Vigneri

Publishing Operations Team
Blake Bergen
Vice President, Publications

Carole Uettwiller
Vice President of Planning and Technology

Robert Methven
Vice President, Digital Publisher

Vince Gallo
Senior Creative Director

Francesca O'Malley
Art/Design Director

Cesar Llacuna
Senior Image Manager

Cheryl Golding
Production Director

Monica Reece
Senior Production Manager

Jovito Pagkalinawan
Electronic Prepress Director

Martin Smith
Planning and Analysis Project Director

Yolanda Miley
Accounts and Permissions Director

Lucy Rotondi
Business Manager

Design/Image Staff
Kevin Butler, Nancy Figueiredo, Stephen Flanagan, Lorraine Forte, Debrah Kaiser, Gabriel Ricci, Bob Schatz, Karen Tully

Production Staff
Robin D'Amato, Carol Lin, Vincent McDonough, Allison Pagkalinawan, Laura Reischour

Photo Credits
age fotostock/Wavebreak Media: vii. Spirit Juice Studios: v, xi, 7A, 7B, 21A, 21B, 35A, 35B, 49A, 49B, 63A, 63B, 77A, 77B.

Acknowledgments
Excerpts from the English translation of *The Roman Missal* © 2010, International Committee on English in the Liturgy, Inc. (ICEL). All rights reserved.

Excerpts from the English translation of the *Catechism of the Catholic Church* for the United States of America, copyright © 1994, United States Catholic Conference, Inc.—Libreria Editrice Vaticana. English translation of the *Catechism of the Catholic Church: Modifications from the Editio Typica* copyright © 1997, United States Catholic Conference, Inc.—Libreria Editrice Vaticana. Used with permission.

Scripture excerpts are taken from the *New American Bible with Revised New Testament and Psalms*. Copyright © 1991, 1986, 1970, Confraternity of Christian Doctrine, Inc. Washington, D.C. Used with permission. All rights reserved. No part of the *New American Bible* may be reproduced by any means without permission in writing from the copyright owner.

Excerpts from the English translation of *Rite of Baptism for Children* © 1969, ICEL; excerpts from the English translation of *Rite of Christian Initiation of Adults* © 1985, ICEL.

Excerpts from *Catholic Household Blessings and Prayers (Revised Edition)* © 1988, 2007, United States Conference of Catholic Bishops, Inc. Washington, D.C. Used with permission. All rights reserved.

English translation of the Lord's Prayer and Apostles' Creed by the International Consultation on English Texts (ICET).

Excerpts from Pope Paul VI, *Constitution on the Sacred Liturgy*, December 4, 1963, and *Dogmatic Constitution on Divine Revelation*, November 18, 1965, copyright © Vatican Publishing House, Libreria Editrice Vaticana.

Excerpt from Pope John Paul II, Apostolic Letter *Dies Domini*, May 31, 1998, copyright © Vatican Publishing House, Libreria Editrice Vaticana.

"Lead Us to the Water" © 1998, Text © 1998, Tom Kendzia. Music © 1998, Tom Kendzia and Gary Daigle. Published by OCP, 5536 NE Hassalo, Portland, OR 97213. All rights reserved. "Rain Down" © 1991, Jaime Cortez. Published by OCP, 5536 NE Hassalo, Portland, OR 97213. Used with permission. All rights reserved. "Lord, Hear My Prayer" by Jim Gibson, tr. by Jaime Cortez Copyright © 2001, GIA Publications, Inc., 7404 S. Mason Ave., Chicago, IL 60638. • www.giamusic.com • 800.442.1358. All rights reserved. Used by permission. "Our God Is Here" © 2001, Chris Muglia. Published by Spirit & Song, a division of OCP. 5536 NE Hassalo, Portland, OR 97213. All rights reserved. Used with permission. *"Pan de Vida"* Text: John 13:1-15; Galatians 3:28-29; Bob Hurd and Pia Moriarty. Text and music © 1988, Bob Hurd and Pia Moriarty. Published by OCP. All rights reserved. "We Are the Body of Christ/*Somos el Cuerpo de Cristo*" Text: Jaime Cortez and Bob Hurd. Text and music © 1994, Jaime Cortez. Published by OCP. All rights reserved.

25 Broadway
New York, NY 10004-1010

ISBN: 978-0-8215-3122-8
5 6 7 8 9 10 11 SHNW 26 25 24 23 22

Contents

Scope and Sequence

Chapter	Words of Faith	Scripture	*Catechism of the Catholic Church*	Liturgy	Ritual	Saint
1. Belonging to the Church	Church Blessed Trinity Mass sacraments sanctifying grace actual grace	Revelation 3:8 Acts of the Apostles 2:1–4, 38–41 *Pentecost*	1083, 1110, 1115–1116, 1131, 1275, 1277, 1279, 1282, 1316, 1318, 1333, 1413	Sacraments of Christian Initiation	Baptismal remembrance **Music:** "Lead Us to the Water" ©1998, Tom Kendzia and Gary Daigle. Published by OCP.	Saint Dominic Savio
2. Gathering to Give Thanks and Praise	worship assembly vestments Lords Day Introductory Rites	Matthew 18:20 Mark 11:8–9 *Jesus' Entry into Jerusalem*	1156–1158, 1171, 1191, 1194, 1193, 1407, 1410	**Mass:** Introductory Rites	Praying with a cross **Music:** "Rain Down" ©1992, Jaime Cortez. Published by OCP.	Saint Maria Guadalupe
3. Celebrating the Liturgy of the Word	Liturgy of the Word psalm Gospel homily Creed Prayer of the Faithful lector Lectionary ambo Book of the Gospels	James 1:22 Matthew 13:3–8, 23 *The Sower and the Seed*	1171, 1194, 1345–1355, 1408	**Mass:** Liturgy of the Word	Prayer of the Faithful **Music:** "Lord, Hear My Prayer" © 2001, Jim Gibson; translated by Jaime Cortez. Published by GIA Publications, Inc.	Saint Benedict
4. Celebrating the Liturgy of the Eucharist	Last Supper altar Liturgy of the Eucharist sacrifice Eucharistic Prayer Consecration paten chalice Real Presence	Luke 22:19 Mark 14:22–24 *The Last Supper*	1333, 1345–1355, 1407, 1408, 1409, 1411, 1412, 1413	**Mass:** Liturgy of the Eucharist: Preparation of the Gifts; Eucharistic Prayer	Blessing with holy water **Music:** "Our God Is Here" © 2001, Chris Muglia. Published by OCP.	Saint Brigid
5. Receiving the Body and Blood of Christ	Holy Communion sign of peace Host	John 6:35 Luke 24:13–35 *Jesus on the Road to Emmaus*		**Mass:** Liturgy of the Eucharist: Communion Rite	Sharing a sign of peace **Music:** "*Pan de Vida*" © 1988, 1995, 1999, Bob Hurd and Pia Moriarty. Published by OCP.	Saint Josephine Bakhita
6. Living as the Body of Christ	Concluding Rites blessing tabernacle Most Blessed Sacrament	John 15:12 Matthew 28:16–20 *The Commissioning of the Disciples*	1416	**Mass:** Concluding Rites	Going forth **Music:** "We Are the Body of Christ/*Somos el Cuerpo de Cristo*" © 1994, 2009, Jaime Cortez and Bob Hurd. Published by OCP.	Saint Pedro Calungsod

Introduction and Philosophy

by Matthew Halbach, Ph.D.

Belief, celebration, and lived faith together nurture and shape the life of the disciple. Belief informs our celebration and our lived experience of faith. Through worship, we celebrate what we believe, and we share those beliefs in sacramental form. Likewise, our own lived experience of faith informs our beliefs and our celebration of faith by orienting them toward the love and service of others. Lived faith is faith in action; it is celebration with the purpose of sharing Christ with others.

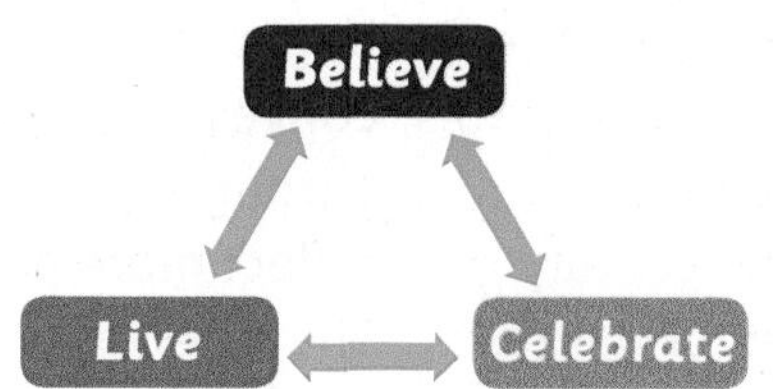

A holistic approach to faith formation includes each of the above elements. All three are found in every chapter of this series. Each chapter begins with the child's lived experience of faith which is then connected through words of Scripture, the liturgy, and the teachings of the Church. The child is then invited to celebrate his or her faith through prayer and song. Finally, and most important, parents and their children are invited to put their faith in action, together, through various activities and service opportunities. Thus, belief, celebration, and our lived experience of faith help to form disciples who know, love, and serve both God and neighbor. Our journey of faith is a call to believe, celebrate, and live. Now let's take a look at the ways that **Believe—Celebrate—Live** can help children respond to this call.

Liturgical Catechesis

by Donna Eschenauer, Ph.D.

Liturgical catechesis recognizes the profound relationship between liturgy and catechesis. This relationship is essential to preparing children for active participation in the celebrations of the Sacraments of Penance and Reconciliation and the Eucharist.

Children have a natural capacity for wonder and awe. They are open to the greatness of God and eager to learn. Developmentally, children experience a profound sense of identity in and through ritual prayer. Their Catholic Identity is shaped and nurtured through ritual activities that appeal to their senses. Within the context of the liturgical year, assembly, song, symbol, Scripture, gesture, and even silence nurture the sacramental imagination of children and offer them deeper insight into the world.

It is important to understand that liturgical catechesis is one aspect of catechesis, rather than an alternative method of catechesis. The purpose of liturgical catechesis is threefold:

- It is catechesis toward the liturgy.
- It is catechesis in and through the liturgy.
- It offers the opportunity for reflection on the liturgical experience.

Believe—Celebrate—Live aims to prepare children to celebrate the sacraments as baptized members of the Body of Christ. The text fosters beliefs that will reveal the mystery of Jesus Christ and the Church and lead to active participation in the liturgy. It promotes service to others in ways that can influence children and families in the lifelong process of learning to see God's presence and action in the world.

Lectio Divina and *Visio Divina*

by Barbara Sutton, D.Min

In this sacramental preparation series we will lead children to hear and see the Word of God through Scripture text and art by using the ancient practice of *Lectio Divina* and its visual counterpart, *Visio Divina*. *Lectio Divina*, the devotional reading of Scripture, was first established in the sixth century by Saint Benedict of Nursia and was later formalized as a four-step process: (1) a slow, meditative reading of the Word of God, (2) pondering the Word, (3) silent listening for God to speak to us through this Word, and (4) listening to our response to God's Word. Through *Visio Divina*, Scripture art is used to ponder the Word visually. *Visio Divina* slows the viewer down, moving one from a typical quick glance to a sacred gaze on Scripture art. When the children engage in this practice, as their gaze deepens, they will begin to notice the deeper meaning conveyed in each Scripture illustration. Through question prompts, they will be led to reflect more deeply on what they are seeing. The catechist's use of open-ended questions will facilitate a seeing that builds a bridge between a child's personal faith story and God's Word.

Lectio Divina and *Visio Divina* help the children to understand Sacred Scripture as the Living Word of God, discovering its deep meaning through word and image.

Ritual Prayer by Tom Kendzia, B.Mus.Ed.

Each of the chapters in this program ends with a ritual prayer. The prayer experience is not intended to "conclude" the lesson catechetically, but to offer an experience of ritual prayer that draws on the rites of the Catholic Church, both sacramentally and liturgically:

- **Structure:** The form of these prayers comes from the actual rites of the Church, mostly from the liturgy of the Mass.
- **Music:** The music selections are pieces of liturgical music found in hymnals used throughout the United States and elsewhere.
- **Symbol:** The symbols used are those we would use at Mass, especially for sacramental celebrations.
- **Gesture:** Gesture and movement are important features of ritual prayer, as they have the unique ability to unify the worshiping community and, in this case, the children gathered to learn and pray together.
- **Environment:** Creating a "sacred place" in a prominent spot in your room is an essential piece of these rituals—again, a direct mirror of our worship space in church.

There are three key components to successful liturgical catechesis:

1. ***We prepare:*** Simply put, we outline what we will be doing (not why or how). This includes rehearsing the music to be sung together. We succinctly mention any gestures or movements, which are usually directed by the leader, the catechist. The tracks on the music CD include enough time for spoken parts over the instrumental music between any refrains to be sung by the group.
2. ***We experience:*** We pray the prayer and accompany it with gestures.
3. ***We respond:*** We ask the children to respond to the experience in a public fashion by answering open-ended questions related to their own experience. This sharing is essential in the growth of the living Body of Christ. With patience and kindness, you can help the children feel comfortable sharing their feelings and reflections, and the experience will be a rewarding one for you and the children!

Celebrating Inclusion

Strategies and tips for including children with disabilities in sacrament preparations and celebrations

by Charleen Katra, M.A.

Celebrating the sacraments is a baptismal right of every Catholic; however, the ways children are best prepared will vary based upon individual learning needs. To make the preparations and celebrations a joyful experience for everyone involved, consider implementing the following practices as needed.

- Provide a "buddy" (i.e., a peer mentor, youth, or young adult) to assist a child who has a disability.
- Teach the process of receiving a sacrament one step at a time, then role-play those steps repeatedly.
- Teach children who have language delays to make "prayer hands" (palms together, fingers pointing up) to indicate "Amen."
- Allow children who have a sensitivity to taste and texture to practice consuming unconsecrated hosts, either whole or a small part.
- Advise the pastor when children with learning differences will be celebrating a sacrament. Provide any specific helpful information regarding the child's special needs, such as any verbal or interpersonal limitations.

When children with disabilities are prepared for and celebrate the sacraments, their entire family's Catholic Identity is affirmed. At the same time, the faith community gives witness to Gospel values of justice and love. To offer intentional support to children who learn differently, review the section titled "Celebrating Inclusion" at the end of each chapter. It provides strategies and tips to successfully include and teach the lesson to diverse learners.

Celebrating Cultural Diversity

Traditions and customs from cultures that make up our one church

by C. Vanessa White, Ph.D.

As the children's understanding of their Catholic Identity continues to develop, helping them to know the diversity of peoples and customs that make up and enrich the Church is essential. To support that development, every chapter of the guide includes a "Celebrating Cultural Diversity" feature that you can read and explore with the children. Each feature connects to the theme of the chapter or to the saint presented in the chapter. Together with the children you will discover devotional and worship practices related to the celebration of the sacraments, Scripture, and the Blessed Virgin Mary and the saints, reflecting cultures around the world, including Latino, Asian, Italian, Filipino, and African. Some cultural customs presented are specific to a particular country or region, while others have become part of the religious expression of the faithful here at home. By engaging the children in learning about diverse Catholic customs, you will affirm their and their families' faith practices and help them open their minds and hearts to the true universality of the Catholic Church.

Program Components

Child's Books

Age-appropriate sacramental preparation that engages young people's religious imagination!

English and Spanish Availability

Resources for ages 7 and 8 in both English and Bilingual editions

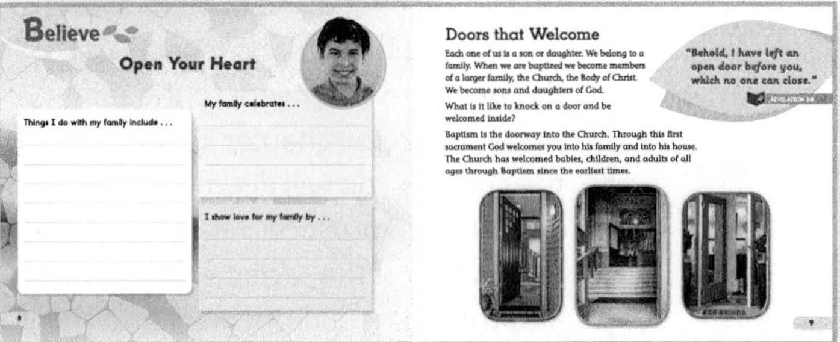

Primary English

Resources for ages 9 and 10 in both English and Spanish editions

Intermediate English

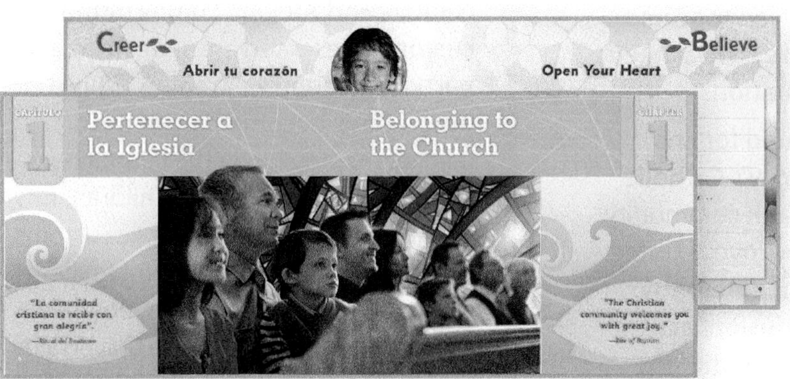

Primary Bilingual

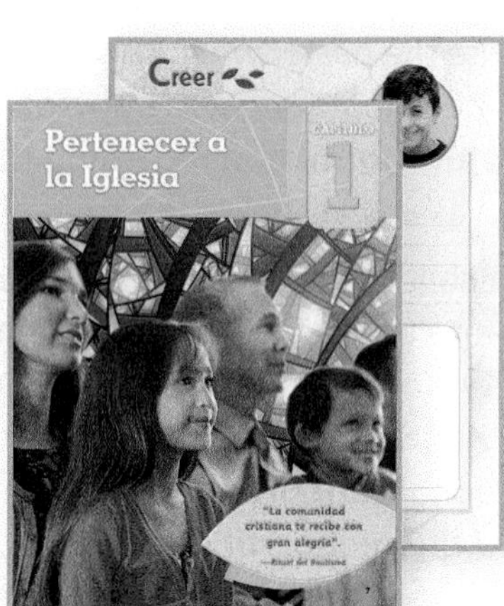

Intermediate Spanish

Catechist Guides

Available in English Primary and Intermediate, Bilingual Primary, and Spanish Intermediate editions

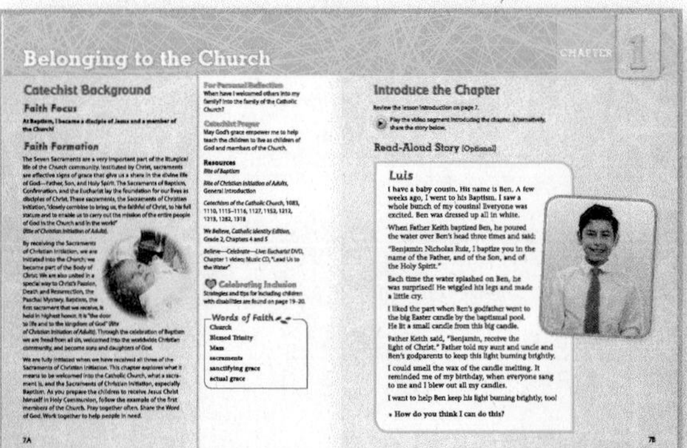

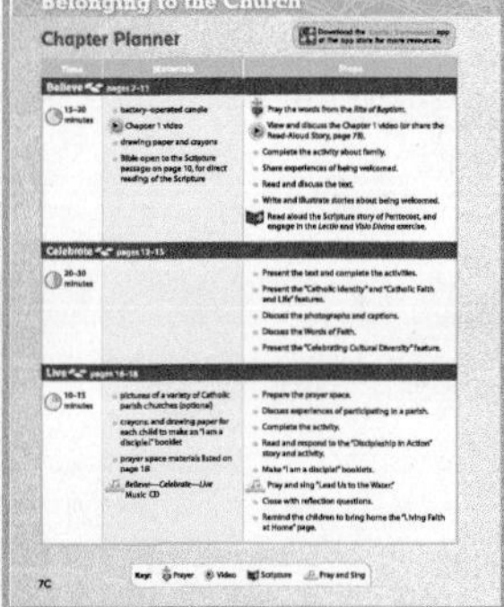

Celebrating Cultural Diversity opens doors to understanding the many cultures that make up our one Church.

Celebrating Inclusion provides strategies and tips for including children with disabilities in sacramental preparation and celebrations.

- Clear planning guide
- Engaging activities

Child's Books, Primary (Ages 7–8)

English and Bilingual

English and Bilingual

English and Bilingual

Child's Books, Intermediate (Ages 9–10)

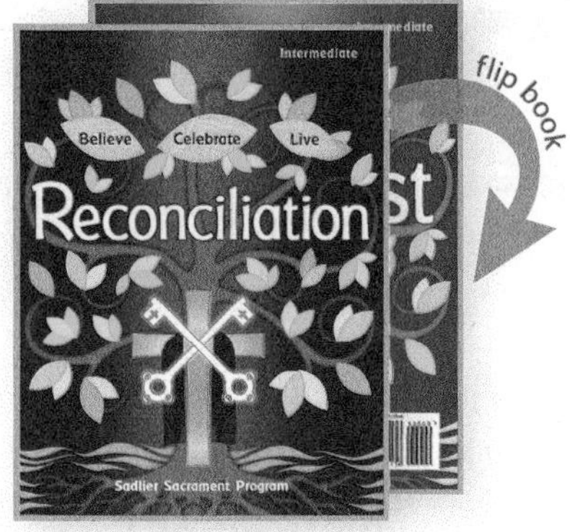

Reconciliation and Eucharist combined in English and Spanish editions

Catechist Guides, Primary

English and Bilingual

English and Bilingual

English and Bilingual

Catechist Guides, Intermediate

Reconciliation and Eucharist English and Spanish

Program Components

DVDs/Videos

Music CDs

Mobile App

for Catechists and Parents

Family Resources

Living Our Faith at Home: Eucharist

Living Our Faith at Home: Reconciliation

Available in English and Spanish

Director's Resource Guide

 eBook

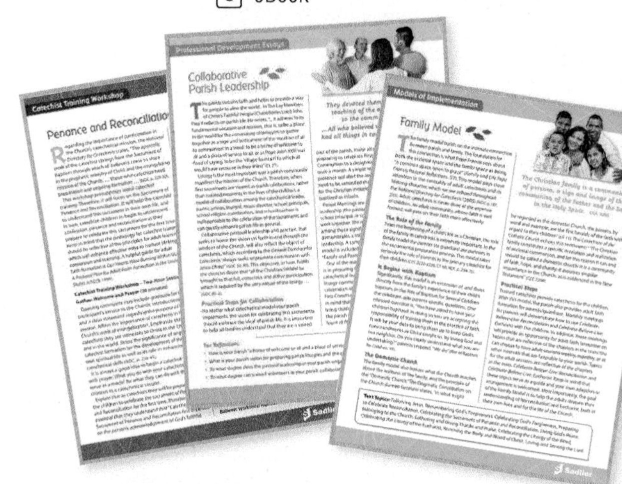

Available in English and Spanish

My Reconciliation & Prayer Book

My Mass Book

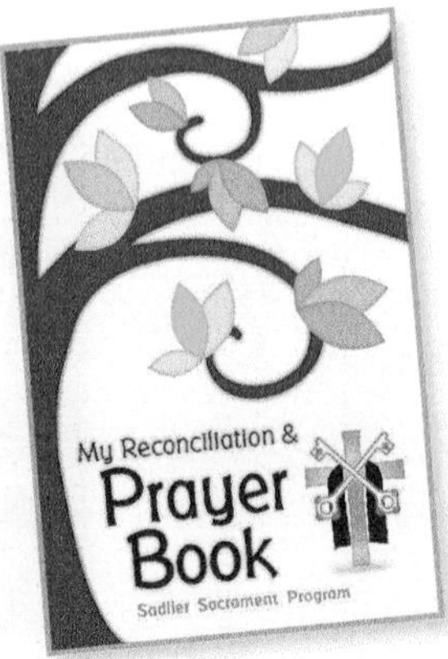

Available in English and Spanish

A Chapter at a Glance

Believe...

Our response to God's love for us is belief. We listen to the Word of the Lord, and it resonates in our hearts and in our lives.

Celebrate...

The Church's liturgical celebrations open the door to an awareness of the Paschal Mystery and a deeper relationship with Jesus Christ. This relationship is nourished through the understanding of Church teachings and practices.

Live...

We become that which we celebrate. The Holy Spirit graces us to answer the ongoing call to conversion by living faith in the world.

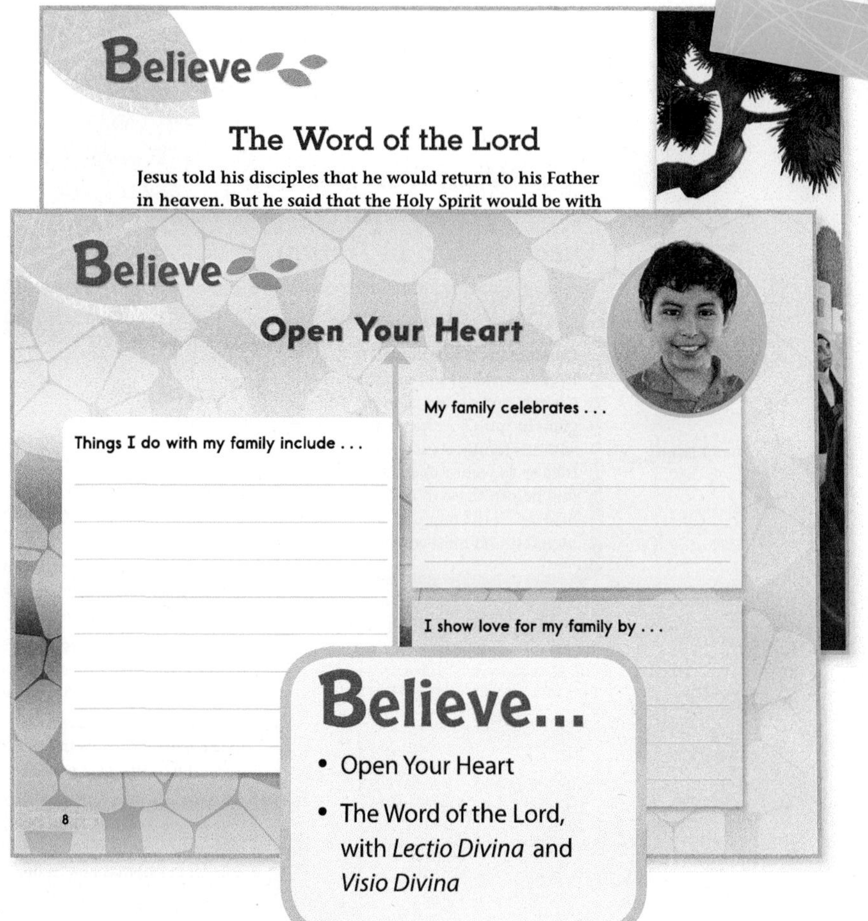

Believe
The Word of the Lord
Jesus told his disciples that he would return to his Father in heaven. But he said that the Holy Spirit would be with
Believe
Open Your Heart
My family celebrates . . .
Things I do with my family include . . .
I show love for my family by . . .
8
Believe...
• Open Your Heart
• The Word of the Lord, with Lectio Divina and Visio Divina

Celebrate

Sacraments of Christian Initiation

Celebrate

The Church

To receive the salvation from sin that Christ offers us, we must be baptized. In Baptism, we become members of Christ and his Church. We die to sin and rise to new life in Christ. ...embers of the Body of Christ and temples of the ...e share in the priesthood of Christ. This is ... for us.

CATHOLIC IDENTITY
At Baptism we become members of the Body of Christ and tem... Holy Spiri...

Captions are used to support content with imagery.

In Baptism, we become a part ... Church. The **Church** is the con... who are baptized and are calle... Christ. The Church is the Body of C... Church we learn and pray together.

As Catholics we believe in the **Blessed Trinity**. The Blessed Trinity is the Three Persons in One God: God the Father, God the Son, and God the Holy Spirit. We believe that Jesus Christ is the Son of God, the Second Person of the Blessed Trinity, who became man. He died and rose from the dead to save, or heal, us from our sins.

12

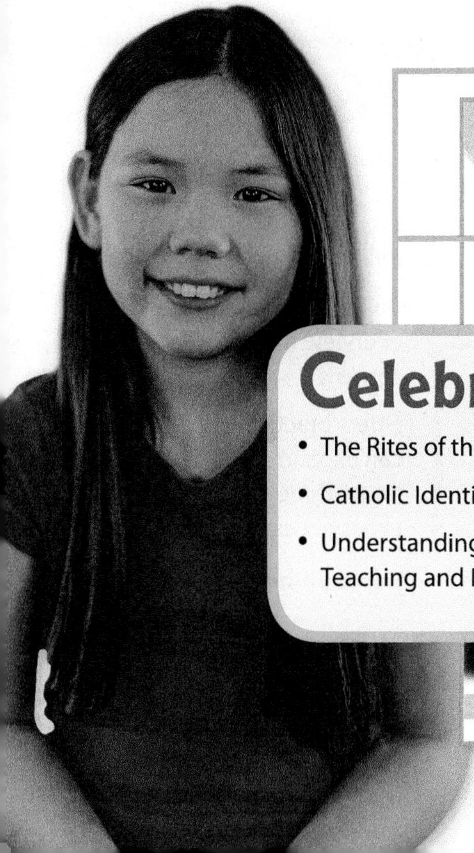

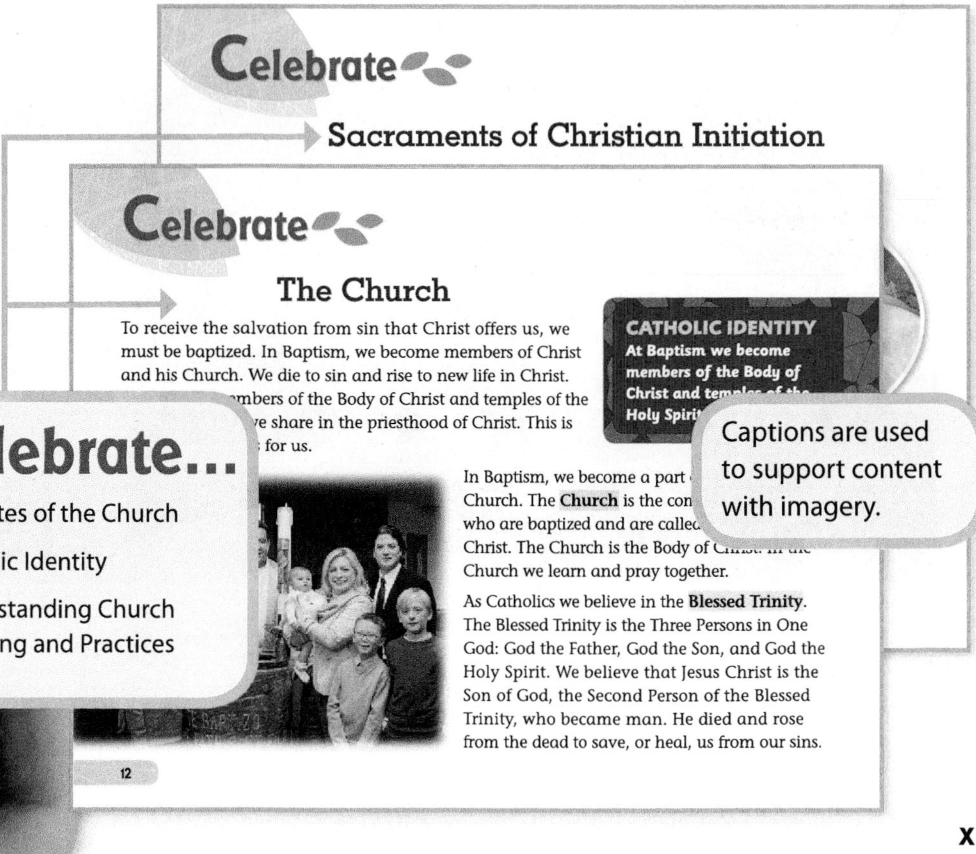

Celebrate...

- The Rites of the Church
- Catholic Identity
- Understanding Church Teaching and Practices

A Chapter at a Glance

Live

Become What You Believe

I am a memb

The pope's n

I was baptiz

Today I belo

Our pastor's

What I like b

16

Discipleship in Action

Saint Dominic Savio (1842–1857)

Dominic Savio was named l
lived in a village in Italy. Hi
Church leaders said Domini
giant in spirit." At home, he
with his family. At school, h
tried to do what was right. H
and helped those in need. V
his First Holy Communion,
happiest and most wonderf

As a disciple I can . . .

Live

Lead Us to the Water

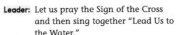

Leader: Let us pray the Sign of the Cross and then sing together "Lead Us to the Water."

All: (*Sing*) Lead us to the water, bring us to the feast. Wash us in the river, and fill us with your peace.

Leader: Lord Jesus, we thank you for the gift of faith. It is you who calls us each by name to become your followers.

All: (*Sing*) Lead us to the water, bring us to the feast. Wash us in the river, and fill us with your peace.

Leader: Lord Jesus, we have heard your call to love one another. From the waters of Baptism we are sent to be your light in our homes and in the world.

All: (*Sing*) Lead us to the water, bring us to the feast. Wash us in the river, and fill us with your peace.

Leader: Come forward to bless yourselves with the holy water from the bowl. Let this water remind us of our Baptism, as we ask Jesus to help us to bring his light and peace to the world.

All: (*Sing*) Lead us to the water, bring us to the feast. Wash us in the river, and fill us with your peace.

Leader: Let us fold our hands and pray as Jesus taught us.

All: Our Father . . .

18

Live...

- Become What You Believe
- Discipleship in Action
- Ritual Prayer, Liturgical Music, and Mystagogical Reflection

Living Faith at Home

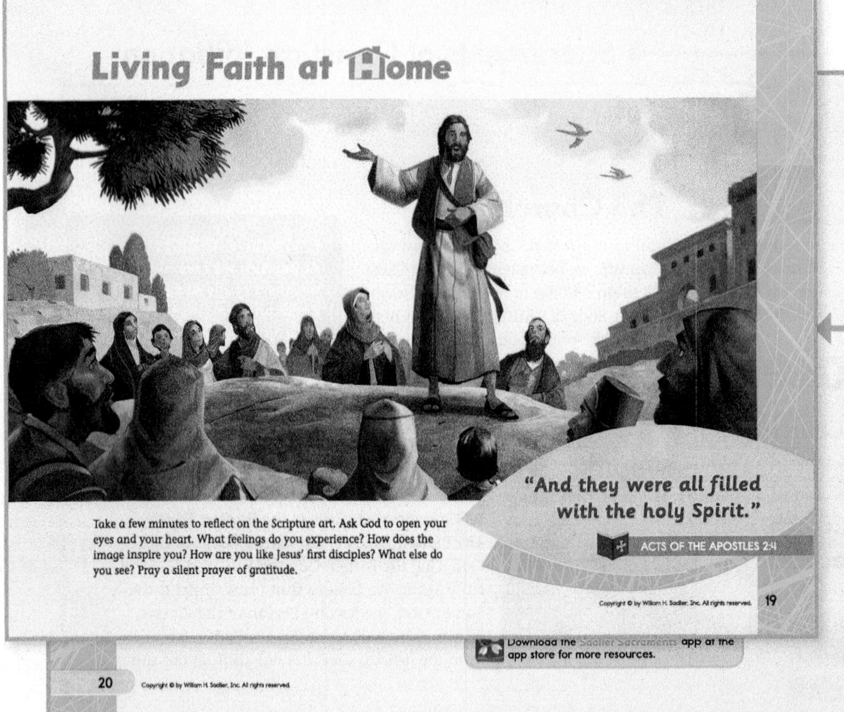

"*And they were all filled with the holy Spirit.*"

ACTS OF THE APOSTLES 2:4

Take a few minutes to reflect on the Scripture art. Ask God to open your eyes and your heart. What feelings do you experience? How does the image inspire you? How are you like Jesus' first disciples? What else do you see? Pray a silent prayer of gratitude.

 19

Download the Sadlier Sacraments app at the app store for more resources.

20

Living Faith at Home

Inspires parents through reflection on the Scripture

Gives parents a quick overview of the chapter content

Offers practical ways parents can expand the chapter at home through everyday experiences

Let's get started!

Eucharist: Parish Church Tour

Help children locate the numbered items in the illustration of a parish church (student text pages 4–5). Give a brief description for each.

1 **sanctuary** the part of the church that includes the altar and the ambo. The word *sanctuary* means "holy place."

2 **altar** the special table that is the center of the celebration of the Liturgy of the Eucharist, also called the Table of the Lord

3 **crucifix** a cross with a figure of Christ crucified, displayed in the sanctuary

4 **tabernacle** the special place in the church in which the Most Blessed Sacrament is placed in reserve

5 **sanctuary lamp** light or candle that is always lit near the tabernacle. It helps us to remember that Jesus is really present in the Most Blessed Sacrament.

6 **ambo** a sacred reading stand called the Table of the Word of God. The ambo is used for the proclamation of the Scripture in the liturgy.

7 **chalice** the special cup into which the priest pours the grape wine that becomes the Blood of Christ during the Liturgy of the Eucharist

8 **paten** the special plate on which the priest places the wheat bread that becomes the Body of Christ during the Liturgy of the Eucharist

9 **cruets** small glass jars that contain the water and the grape wine used at Mass

10 **presider's chair** chair on which the priest who is celebrating Mass sits

11 **processional cross** cross with a figure of Christ crucified that is carried in the entrance procession and may also be carried during the Offertory procession and during the recessional

12 **Paschal Candle** a large candle that is blessed and lit every Easter. The lighted Paschal Candle represents the Risen Christ among us. The flame of the Paschal Candle is used to light baptismal candles.

13 **baptismal font or pool** contains the water that is blessed and used during the Sacrament of Baptism

14 **Stations of the Cross** fourteen pictures that help us to follow the footsteps of Jesus during his Passion and Death on the Cross

15 **Reconciliation Room or confessional** a separate space for celebrating the Sacrament of Penance and Reconciliation. This is where you meet the priest for individual confession and absolution. You may sit and talk to him face to-face or kneel behind a screen.

16 **stained glass** colorful windows that may show saints or scenes from Scripture

17 **pews** where the assembly is seated during the celebration of Mass

18 **statue of Mary** image of the Mother of God, our greatest saint; statues of other saints may also be found in the church.

Belonging to the Church

Catechist Background

Faith Focus

At Baptism, I became a disciple of Jesus and a member of the Church!

Faith Formation

The Seven Sacraments are a very important part of the liturgical life of the Church community. Instituted by Christ, sacraments are effective signs of grace that give us a share in the divine life of God—Father, Son, and Holy Spirit. The Sacraments of Baptism, Confirmation, and the Eucharist lay the foundation for our lives as disciples of Christ. These sacraments, the Sacraments of Christian Initiation, "closely combine to bring us, the faithful of Christ, to his full stature and to enable us to carry out the mission of the entire people of God in the Church and in the world" (*Rite of Christian Initiation of Adults*).

By receiving the Sacraments of Christian Initiation, we are initiated into the Church; we become part of the Body of Christ. We are also united in a special way to Christ's Passion, Death and Resurrection, the Paschal Mystery. Baptism, the first sacrament that we receive, is held in highest honor. It is "the door to life and to the kingdom of God" (*Rite of Christian Initiation of Adults*). Through the celebration of Baptism we are freed from all sin, welcomed into the worldwide Christian community, and become sons and daughters of God.

We are fully initiated when we have received all three of the Sacraments of Christian Initiation. This chapter explores what it means to be welcomed into the Catholic Church, what a sacrament is, and the Sacraments of Christian Initiation, especially Baptism. As you prepare the children to receive Jesus Christ himself in Holy Communion, follow the example of the first members of the Church. Pray together often. Share the Word of God. Work together to help people in need.

For Personal Reflection

When have I welcomed others into my family? into the family of the Catholic Church?

Catechist Prayer

May God's grace empower me to help teach the children to live as children of God and members of the Church.

Resources

Rite of Baptism

Rite of Christian Initiation of Adults, General Introduction

Catechism of the Catholic Church, 1083, 1110, 1115–1116, 1127, 1152, 1212, 1213, 1282, 1318

We Believe, Catholic Identity Edition, Grade 2, Chapters 4 and 5

Believe—Celebrate—Live: Eucharist DVD, Chapter 1 video; Music CD, "Lead Us to the Water"

Celebrating Inclusion

Strategies and tips for including children with disabilities are found on page 19–20.

Words of Faith

Church

Blessed Trinity

Mass

sacraments

sanctifying grace

actual grace

Introduce the Chapter

Review the lesson introduction on page 7.

Play the video segment introducing the chapter. Alternatively, share the story below.

Read-Aloud Story (Optional)

Luis

I have a baby cousin. His name is Ben. A few weeks ago, I went to his Baptism. I saw a whole bunch of my cousins! Everyone was excited. Ben was dressed up all in white.

When Father Keith baptized Ben, he poured the water over Ben's head three times and said:

"Benjamin Nicholas Ruiz, I baptize you in the name of the Father, and of the Son, and of the Holy Spirit."

Each time the water splashed on Ben, he was surprised! He wiggled his legs and made a little cry.

I liked the part when Ben's godfather went to the big Easter candle by the baptismal pool. He lit a small candle from this big candle.

Father Keith said, "Benjamin, receive the light of Christ." Father told my aunt and uncle and Ben's godparents to keep this light burning brightly.

I could smell the wax of the candle melting. It reminded me of my birthday, when everyone sang to me and I blew out all my candles.

I want to help Ben keep his light burning brightly, too!

- **How do you think I can do this?**

Belonging to the Church

Chapter Planner

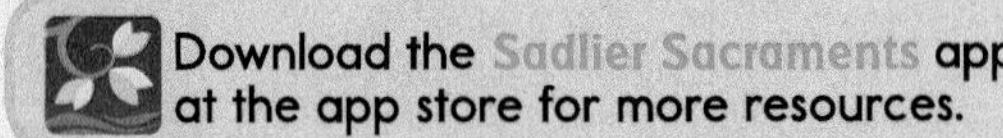
Download the Sadlier Sacraments app at the app store for more resources.

Time	Materials	Steps
Believe pages 7–11		
15–20 minutes	• battery-operated candle Chapter 1 video • drawing paper and crayons • Bible open to the Scripture passage on page 10, for direct reading of the Scripture	Pray the words from the *Rite of Baptism*. View and discuss the Chapter 1 video (or share the Read-Aloud Story, page 7B). • Complete the activity about family. • Share experiences of being welcomed. • Read and discuss the text. • Write and illustrate stories about being welcomed. Read aloud the Scripture story of Pentecost, and engage in the *Lectio* and *Visio Divina* exercise.
Celebrate pages 12–15		
20–30 minutes		• Present the text and complete the activities. • Present the "Catholic Identity" and "Catholic Faith and Life" features. • Discuss the photographs and captions. • Discuss the Words of Faith. • Present the "Celebrating Cultural Diversity" feature.
Live pages 16–18		
10–15 minutes	• pictures of a variety of Catholic parish churches (optional) • crayons and drawing paper for each child to make an "I am a disciple!" booklet • prayer space materials listed on page 18 *Believe—Celebrate—Live* Music CD	• Prepare the prayer space. • Discuss experiences of participating in a parish. • Complete the activity. • Read and respond to the "Discipleship in Action" story and activity. • Make "I am a disciple!" booklets. Pray and sing "Lead Us to the Water." • Close with reflection questions. • Remind the children to bring home the "Living Faith at Home" page.

Key: Prayer 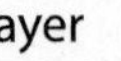 Video  Scripture 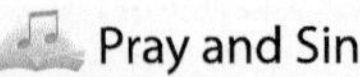 Pray and Sing

Introduce the Chapter

Belonging to the Church

Welcome the children and express your joy in being part of their journey with Jesus.

Gather for prayer. Light a battery-operated candle. Then pray together the Sign of the Cross. Call attention to the verse on page 7, from the *Rite of Baptism*. Proclaim the words together.

Share that at our Baptism, each of us is "claimed for Christ" and becomes a member of the Christian family. At the end of the rite, the priest says, "The Christian community welcomes you with great joy." Our new family is joyful because of the gifts we bring to our Christian community.

Share that a family is a community—a group of people who share with one another, work together, and care for one another.

Direct attention to the photograph on this page.

Ask *Where do you think the family is? Does everyone look happy? Why do you think they feel that way?*

Introduce the video segment for this chapter by saying, "Let's explore some of the themes of this chapter with our young friends from the chapter video." Play the video.

Alternatively, you may choose to share the Read-Aloud Story found on page 7B of this guide.

Notes ______________________________

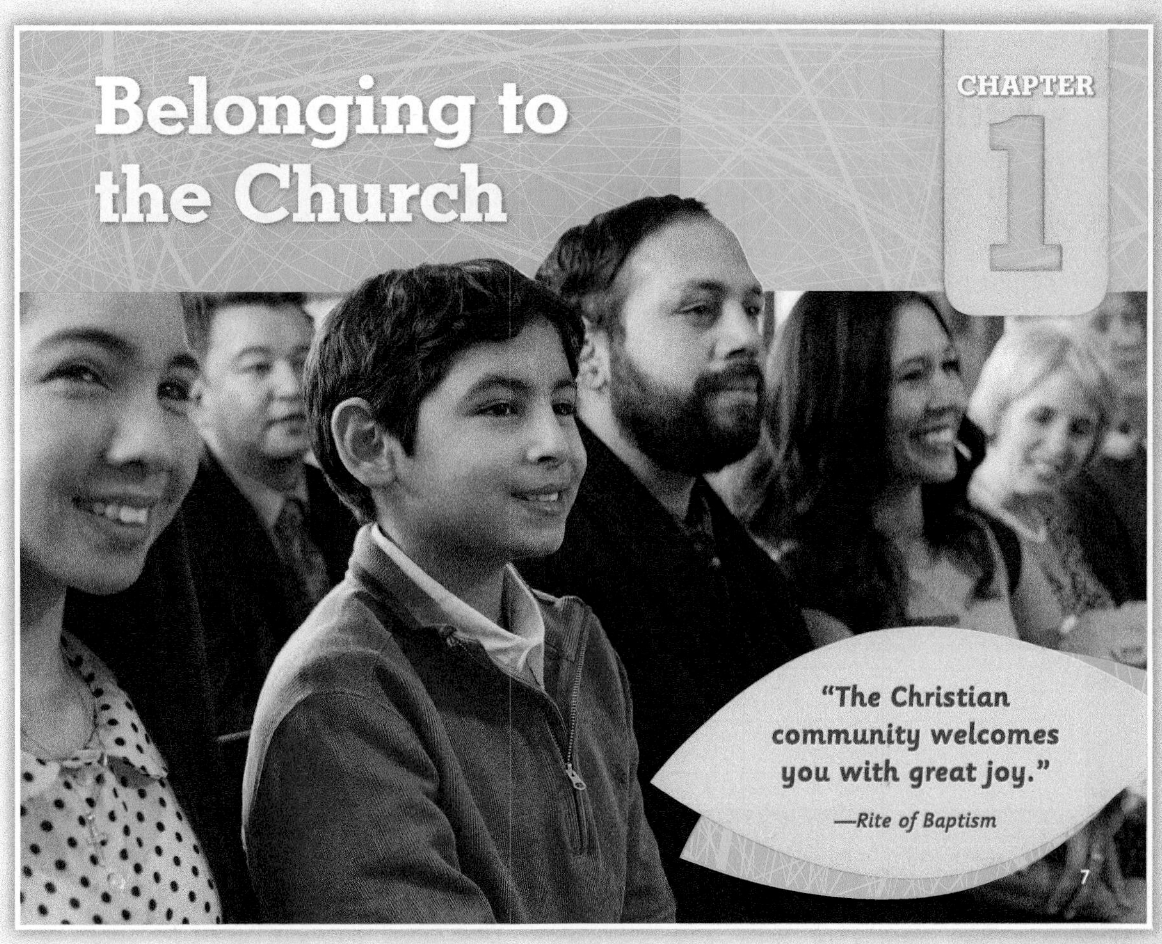
Belonging to the Church
CHAPTER
1
"The Christian community welcomes you with great joy."
—Rite of Baptism
7

Believe

Open Your Heart

Ask the children the following or similar questions about what they saw in the video or heard in the Read-Aloud Story:

When did you become part of God's family?

What does it mean to be part of God's family?

What did you see or hear that was different or new to you?

Explain "You are a gift from God, just by being you!"

Invite the children to think about their family at home. Explain that families may look different, but God is a part of every family. You may wish to share with the children what your family is like. Explain that our families help us to be followers of Jesus.

Activity

Have the children look at the sentence starters. Invite them to tell about their family by completing the sentences.

Things I do with my family include . . .
Have the children write their favorite activities or special times spent with their family. These might include things they do every day or special memories, such as vacations or family outings.

My family celebrates . . .
Ask the children to name their favorite family celebrations, such as birthdays, holidays, or the celebration of a sacrament.

I show love for my family by . . .
Before the children complete this sentence, invite them to talk about why their family is special.

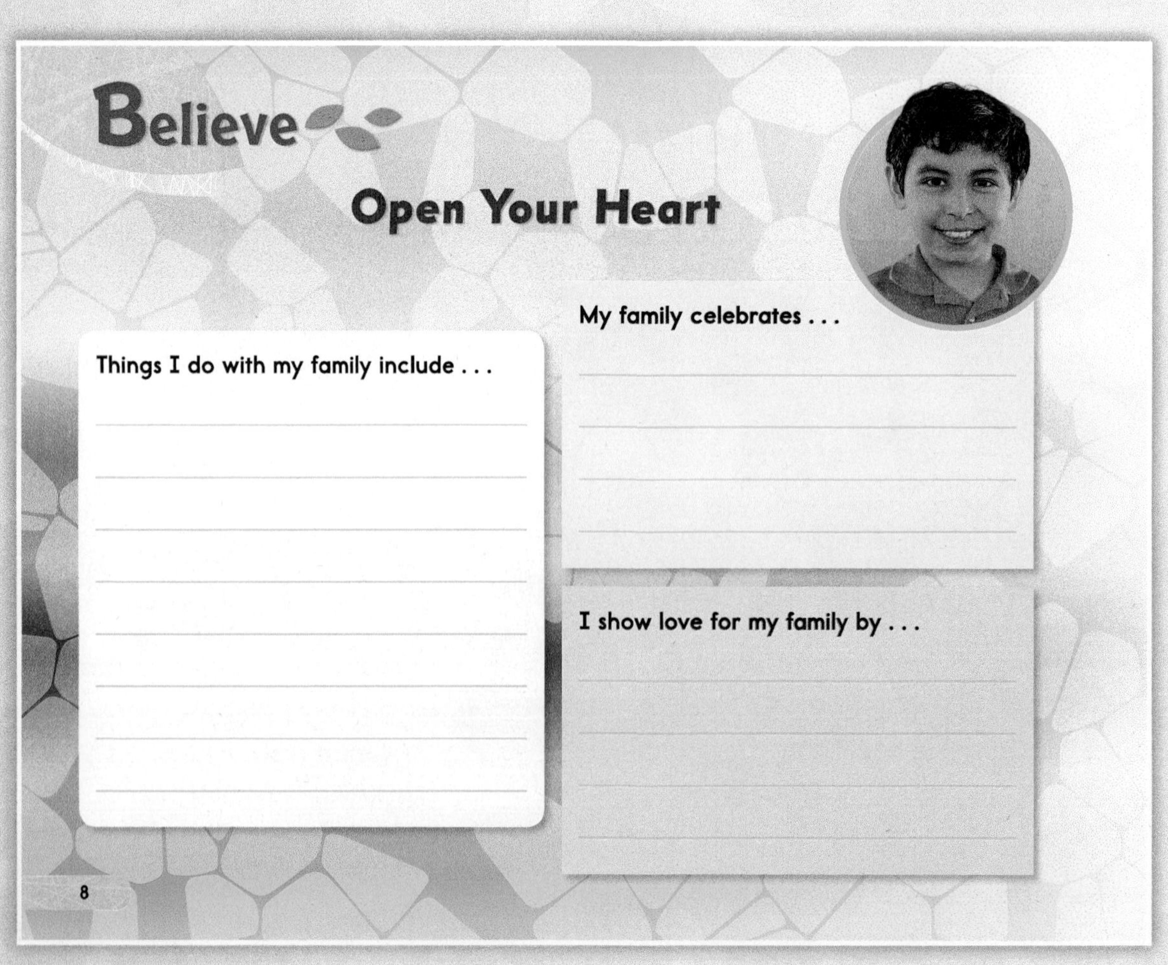
Believe
Open Your Heart
My family celebrates . . .
Things I do with my family include . . .
I show love for my family by . . .
8

Doors that Welcome

Share with the children a time when you were welcomed somewhere new. Have them recall a time when they experienced being welcomed. Invite them to share their experience with a partner.

Direct attention to the images of doors. Present the first paragraph.

Ask *What is it like to knock on a door and be welcomed inside?*

Read the Scripture quote from the Book of Revelation together. Ask the children what they think the quote means. Explain that God himself invites us to be his children forever.

Read the last paragraph.

Ask *What does it mean that Baptism is the doorway into the Church? How do we know that God wants us to be part of his family?*

Activity

Help the children relate what they have read to personal experience. Have the children imagine that they are going somewhere new and don't know many people there.

- Ask the children: *Where are you going? What are you thinking about before you arrive? What do people do or say to make you feel welcome?*
- Distribute drawing materials. Ask the children to write a story about their experience and to draw pictures to go with it. Invite them to share their stories with the group.

Notes ______________________

____

____

____

Doors that Welcome

Each one of us is a son or daughter. We belong to a family. When we are baptized we become members of a larger family, the Church, the Body of Christ. We become sons and daughters of God.

What is it like to knock on a door and be welcomed inside?

"Behold, I have left an open door before you, which no one can close."

REVELATION 3:8

Baptism is the doorway into the Church. Through this first sacrament God welcomes you into his family and into his house. The Church has welcomed babies, children, and adults of all ages through Baptism since the earliest times.

Believe

The Word of the Lord

Share that disciples are followers of Jesus. Jesus and his disciples were like a family. They cared about one another and shared with others.

Read aloud the introductory paragraph before the Scripture.

Explain that the children are going to listen to a reading from the Bible, the living Word of God. The Scripture reading explains what happened to the community of Jesus' disciples about ten days after Jesus returned to his Father in heaven.

Guide the children through an adaptation of *Lectio Divina*, a special way to pray with Scripture. Quiet the children, and ask them to listen carefully to the Scripture reading as you read it aloud.

Reflect on the reading by inviting the children to:

- Take a moment to think about what they heard.
- Silently answer the following questions for reflection (be sure to pause after each question): *What word or words did you hear? What do you think Jesus is saying to you?*
- Quietly hold these words in their hearts. (Pause in prayer.)
- Share aloud in one or two words what they heard. Describe what they were feeling in their hearts. (Accept all responses.)

Guide the children through an adaptation of *Visio Divina*, a special way to pray with Scripture art. Quiet the children and invite them to take their time looking at the illustration on pages 10 and 11. Read aloud the Scripture once again. Invite the children to silently answer these questions: *What do you see? What does it mean to you? What do you imagine Jesus inviting you to see? What do you think this means for you?*

The Word of the Lord

Jesus told his disciples that he would return to his Father in heaven. But he said that the Holy Spirit would be with them to guide them. The Holy Spirit would help them remember everything that Jesus had said and done.

 Based on ACTS OF THE APOSTLES 2:1–4, 38–41

Jesus' first disciples and Mary, the Mother of Jesus, were gathered together in a room because they were afraid. Suddenly they heard a noise. It sounded like a strong wind. They saw what looked like a flame of fire over each one of them.

"And they were all filled with the holy Spirit." (Acts of the Apostles 2:4)

They left the room. Then Peter, one of Jesus' Apostles, began teaching. He also invited the people to be baptized. Peter said that they, too, would receive the Gift of the Holy Spirit.

"Those who accepted his message were baptized, and about three thousand persons were added that day." (Acts of the Apostles 2:41)

10

Share After the silent reflection, allow time for sharing aloud responses to these questions. Then invite the children to look again at the picture and silently answer the questions: *What are some things this picture tells you about Pentecost? What does it tell you about what the disciples saw, heard, or felt? How?* Invite volunteers to share their responses aloud.

Check comprehension by asking the following questions:

How did Jesus take care of his disciples after he returned to God the Father? (Jesus sent the Holy Spirit to be with his disciples.)

How did the Holy Spirit help Peter and the others? (The Holy Spirit helped them to be brave enough to leave where they were staying. They began to teach about Jesus and invited people to be baptized.)

Scripture Background

After Pentecost, the baptized followers of Jesus lived in a way that was different from the way other people lived. Jesus' followers prayed every day. They learned about Jesus from Peter and the other Apostles. With the help of the Holy Spirit, they shared Jesus' love with others and also shared what they had with people in need. Because of the special way Jesus' followers lived, many other people wanted to join their community and become members of the Church.

Notes ____________________________

Celebrate

The Church

Share that Baptism welcomes us into God's family. By receiving the Holy Spirit, we can strive to follow Jesus' example in our own lives.

Read aloud page 12. Then ask the children what they think it means to be "a child of God." *What kind of relationship does this mean we have with God?* Point out what Catholics believe:

- The Blessed Trinity is Three Persons in One God: God the Father, God the Son, and God the Holy Spirit.
- Jesus Christ, the Son of God, died and rose to save us.
- At Baptism we become children of God and members of the Church.

Direct attention to the photographs on pages 12 and 13. Emphasize that the people shown in these photographs are followers of Jesus. They are members of the Church.

Activity

Teach the definition of *Church* with the following verses and accompanying actions.

The Church is you.
(Point right hand at people nearby.)

The Church is me.
(Point right hand toward yourself.)

The Church is a worldwide community.
(Spread arms out at sides and open hands.)

CATHOLIC IDENTITY

Read the statement together. Pray aloud: *May the Holy Spirit help us to live joyfully and faithfully as the children of God and members of the Church.*

Celebrate

The Church

To receive the salvation from sin that Christ offers us, we must be baptized. In Baptism, we become members of Christ and his Church. We die to sin and rise to new life in Christ. We become members of the Body of Christ and temples of the Holy Spirit, and we share in the priesthood of Christ. This is what Christ wants for us.

CATHOLIC IDENTITY
At Baptism we become members of the Body of Christ and temples of the Holy Spirit.

In Baptism, we become a part of the Catholic Church. The **Church** is the community of people who are baptized and are called to follow Jesus Christ. The Church is the Body of Christ. In the Church we learn and pray together.

As Catholics we believe in the **Blessed Trinity**. The Blessed Trinity is the Three Persons in One God: God the Father, God the Son, and God the Holy Spirit. We believe that Jesus Christ is the Son of God, the Second Person of the Blessed Trinity, who became man. He died and rose from the dead to save, or heal, us from our sins.

12

Read the text on page 13. Stress that we gather with our parish community to worship God and to share and celebrate God's love. Express excitement about the fact that members of the Catholic Church live in countries all over the world.

Ask for examples of times when the parish community gathers, such as for the celebration of the Eucharist, also called the Mass; the celebration of the other sacraments; for parish events; and to help people in need. Include occasions that are specific to your parish community. You may want to use a parish bulletin as a guide.

Words of Faith

Church (page 12)
Blessed Trinity (page 12)
Mass (page 13)

Celebrating Cultural Diversity

Traditions and customs from cultures that make up our one Church

In many Latino cultures, three important traditions celebrate God's gift of children. *El Bautismo* (the Sacrament of Baptism) binds the child to God and the Church and also publicly affirms the parents' and godparents' commitment to raise the child in the faith. *La presentación del Niño* (the Presentation of the Child) is celebrated within forty days after the birth of a child or when the child is aged three. Celebrated during the liturgy, this ceremony involves a simple blessing and anointing. *La Quinceañera* marks a girl's coming of age at her fifteenth birthday. It is usually celebrated with a Mass or a blessing held in the parish church.

Parish communities gather to worship.

In the Church we are called to love God and others the way Jesus did. We can do this with the help of the Holy Spirit.

There are members of the Catholic Church all over the world. Catholics gather together as parish communities to worship God and to share and celebrate God's love, especially on Sundays. We gather to celebrate the Eucharist, also called the **Mass**, and the other sacraments. We gather to show our love for God and others. We show reverence, or honor and respect, to God. He is our Creator and Father who sent his only Son, Jesus Christ, to save us from sin and help us to live as God's children.

Celebrate

Sacraments of Christian Initiation

Read together the first paragraph on page 14. Emphasize how wonderful it is to be united with Jesus as we celebrate a sacrament.

Share that Baptism is the first sacrament we receive. Read together the next paragraph. Emphasize that we receive the gift of God's grace when we celebrate the Sacrament of Baptism.

Direct attention to the photograph of a baby being baptized. Explain that many people are baptized when they are babies, but older children and adults may also be baptized. These Baptisms are usually celebrated at the "greatest and noblest" Eucharistic liturgy, the Easter Vigil, which is celebrated on Holy Saturday night.

Share that Baptism can be celebrated in two ways:

- pouring water over the head of the person being baptized
- immersion, which means "being placed in water." The priest or deacon can immerse, or plunge, the person completely in water three times. Churches today may have baptismal fonts in the form of a pool, large enough for immersion.

Share that the words of Baptism are always the same. The priest or deacon calls the person's name and says, "I baptize you in the name of the Father, and of the Son, and of the Holy Spirit."

Activity

On Sunday or the next time you visit the church together, point out the baptismal pool or font to the children.

Celebrate

Sacraments of Christian Initiation

The **sacraments** are special signs given to us by Jesus through which we share in God's life and love. The Church celebrates Seven Sacraments. Every time the Church celebrates a sacrament, Jesus is with us through the power of the Holy Spirit. On earth Jesus shared his life with his disciples, through his words and actions. In the sacraments, he shares his life with us, his disciples today. God's life in us makes us holy. We call God's life in us grace. The gift of grace that we receive in the sacraments is **sanctifying grace**. Grace is also at work in our daily lives through **actual grace**.

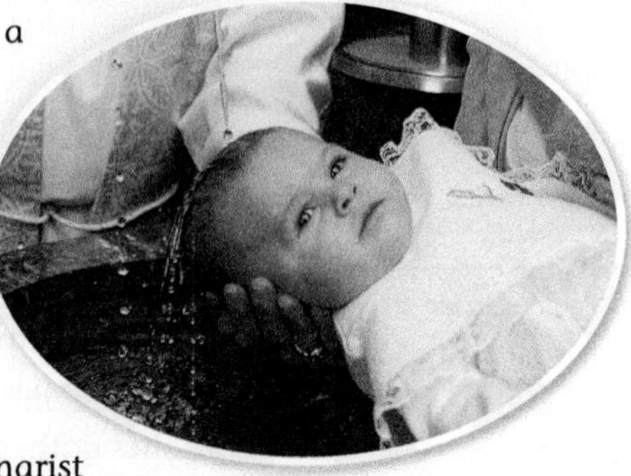

No one is ever too young or too old to receive new life in Christ. It is truly a gift, not something we earn.

The Sacraments of Baptism, Confirmation, and Eucharist are the foundation of our lives as Jesus' disciples. Baptism is the first sacrament we receive. Original Sin and any sins we have personally committed are taken away. We become children of God and members of the Church. At Baptism, the priest or deacon places us in water, which is blessed, or pours the water over our heads.

Explain that, to receive the salvation from sin that Christ offers us, we must be baptized, becoming members of Christ and his Church. In Baptism, the pouring of or immersion into water symbolizes that we die to sin and rise to new life in Christ. In the waters of Baptism, Original Sin and any sins we have personally committed are taken away. We become members of the Body of Christ and temples of the Holy Spirit, and we share in the priesthood of Christ.

Direct attention to the photograph of the Confirmation celebration on page 15. Read aloud the first paragraph. Note that being sealed by the Holy Spirit means that at Confirmation, baptismal grace is enriched and the Holy Spirit is with us in a special way. We become more like Jesus and are strengthened to be his disciples.

Share that the Mass is the celebration of the Sacrament of the Eucharist, which is the "source and summit" of the Christian life. In the Sacrament of the Eucharist we remember Jesus' Death and Resurrection. Emphasize that Jesus is truly present in the Eucharist and that when Catholics receive Holy Communion at Mass, we receive the Body and Blood of Jesus Christ himself under the appearances of bread and wine. Direct attention to the photograph of the child receiving Holy Communion as you read aloud the second paragraph.

Read aloud the last paragraph on page 15.

Catholic Faith and Life

Direct attention to the feature about the Eastern Catholic Churches and the Sacraments of Christian Initiation. Explain that these sacraments are connected to one another, each bringing us more deeply into the Christian life.

Words of Faith

sacraments (page 14)

sanctifying grace (page 14)

actual grace (page 14)

The priest or deacon baptizes us in the name of the Father, the Son, and the Holy Spirit. He anoints us with oil, a sign of the Gift of the Holy Spirit we receive for the first time. In Confirmation, a bishop anoints us with oil. This shows we are sealed with the Gift of the Holy Spirit and strengthened to live as disciples of Jesus.

In the Sacrament of the Eucharist, the whole Church remembers Jesus' Death and Resurrection.

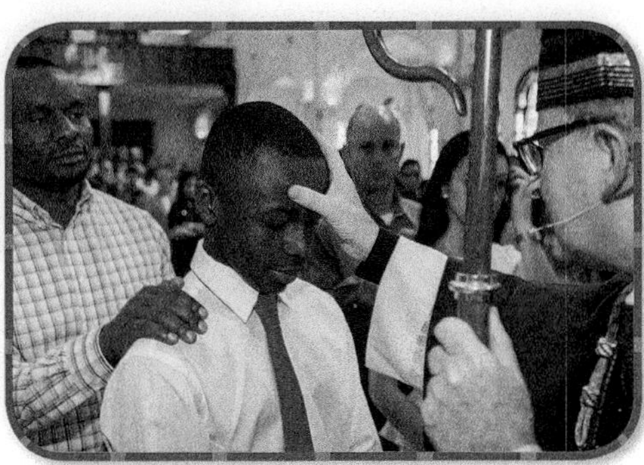

Confirmation seals us with the Gift of the Holy Spirit.

In Eastern Catholic Churches, the Sacraments of Christian Initiation are celebrated together: first Baptism, then Confirmation, then Eucharist. This practice shows the unity of these three sacraments.

When we receive Holy Communion, we receive the Body and Blood, soul and divinity, of Jesus Christ.

The Eucharist is the center of our life. In the Eucharist the bread and wine become the Body and Blood of Jesus Christ. We receive Jesus Christ himself in Holy Communion.

Live

Become What You Believe

Read together the first sentence on page 16. Remind the children that a parish is a family. Invite them to name the parish(es) to which they belong.

Invite the children to discuss their experiences in their parish. You may wish to ask: *What does your parish look like? What things have you done with your parish? Who are your parish priests and deacons?*

Be aware that the children may belong to different parishes. Remind them that all parish families gather to give thanks to God and share his love with others.

Point out the statement in bold at the bottom of the page. Ask the group to read it aloud together and think about what it means in their lives.

Activity

Invite the children to complete the sentence starters. To help them get started you may wish to:

- show pictures of a variety of Catholic parish churches
- have the children recall a celebration in their parish, such as a Baptism or a wedding.

Encourage the children to share their work with the group.

Notes ______________________

____

____

____

____

Live

Become What You Believe

I am a member of the Catholic Church.

The pope's name is ______________________.

I was baptized in ______________________ Parish.

Today I belong to ______________________ Parish.

Our pastor's name is ______________________.

What I like best about my parish is . . .

____

____

____

What makes my parish special is . . .

____

____

____

At Baptism, I became a disciple of Jesus and a member of the Church!

16

Discipleship in Action

Read the story of Saint Dominic Savio on page 17. Explain that Dominic Savio is a saint, a Catholic role model who lived a life very close to Jesus. Saints are Catholic superheroes whose example helps us to live holy lives. Saints like Dominic Savio are part of our Catholic family.

Share that we can be disciples just like Dominic Savio. Have the children share a few ways they can live as disciples.

Notes ______________________________

____

____

____

____

Activity

Have the children complete the "Discipleship in Action" activity. To help them get started, talk about some everyday ways children their age live as followers of Jesus. Then invite each child to make an "I am a disciple!" booklet. Give each child crayons and drawing paper to fold into a booklet. Provide the following instructions:

- Think of the gifts and talents God has given you. How can you best use your gifts and talents to love God and share God's love with others?
- On the inside of the booklet write ways you can be a loving disciple.
- Decorate the cover of your booklet with ways you can show that you are a disciple of Jesus and part of the Catholic family.

Discipleship in Action

Saint Dominic Savio (1842–1857)

Dominic Savio was named Domenico Savio at his Baptism. He lived in a village in Italy. His name means "belonging to God." Church leaders said Dominic was "small in size, but a towering giant in spirit." At home, he prayed and said grace at mealtime with his family. At school, he studied hard. Dominic always tried to do what was right. He stopped his friends from fighting and helped those in need. Whenever Dominic spoke about his First Holy Communion, he said with joy, "That was the happiest and most wonderful day of my life!"

As a disciple I can . . .

____

____

____

____

Live

Lead Us to the Water 

Read and familiarize yourself with the prayer and the music selection. To prepare the environment, arrange the following items on a small table:

- white tablecloth
- glass bowl half full of holy water
- baptismal candle in holder near bowl
- Bible on a table stand

You will also need:

- CD player
- Music CD queued to play track "Lead Us to the Water"

Invite the children to gather around the table with their books. Teach them the song "Lead Us to the Water." Ask the children to quiet themselves for prayer. Briefly describe the ritual action in the prayer—blessing ourselves with holy water. Ask the children to watch when you bless yourself with the water in the bowl and to follow your example. Pray the prayer together, ending with the Lord's Prayer (page 93 of child's book).

Conclude the prayer ritual with the following "mystagogy," or reflection on the experience. Invite the children to give one- or two-word responses to the following:

- *What feeling did you have as you blessed yourself with holy water?*
- *What words from the song or prayer do you remember most?*
- *What is it like for you to be called a follower of Jesus?*

Live

Lead Us to the Water 

Leader: Let us pray the Sign of the Cross and then sing together "Lead Us to the Water."

All: (*Sing*) Lead us to the water, bring us to the feast. Wash us in the river, and fill us with your peace.

Leader: Lord Jesus, we thank you for the gift of faith. It is you who calls us each by name to become your followers.

All: (*Sing*) Lead us to the water, bring us to the feast. Wash us in the river, and fill us with your peace.

Leader: Lord Jesus, we have heard your call to love one another. From the waters of Baptism we are sent to be your light in our homes and in the world.

All: (*Sing*) Lead us to the water, bring us to the feast. Wash us in the river, and fill us with your peace.

Leader: Come forward to bless yourselves with the holy water from the bowl. Let this water remind us of our Baptism, as we ask Jesus to help us to bring his light and peace to the world.

All: (*Sing*) Lead us to the water, bring us to the feast. Wash us in the river, and fill us with your peace.

Leader: Let us fold our hands and pray as Jesus taught us.

All: Our Father . . .

Living Faith at Home

Encourage family participation by having the children take home the double-sided "Living Faith at Home" page.

Living Faith at Home

"And they were all filled with the holy Spirit."

ACTS OF THE APOSTLES 2:4

Take a few minutes to reflect on the Scripture art. Ask God to open your eyes and your heart. What feelings do you experience? How does the image inspire you? How are you like Jesus' first disciples? What else do you see? Pray a silent prayer of gratitude.

Copyright © by William H. Sadlier, Inc. All rights reserved. 19

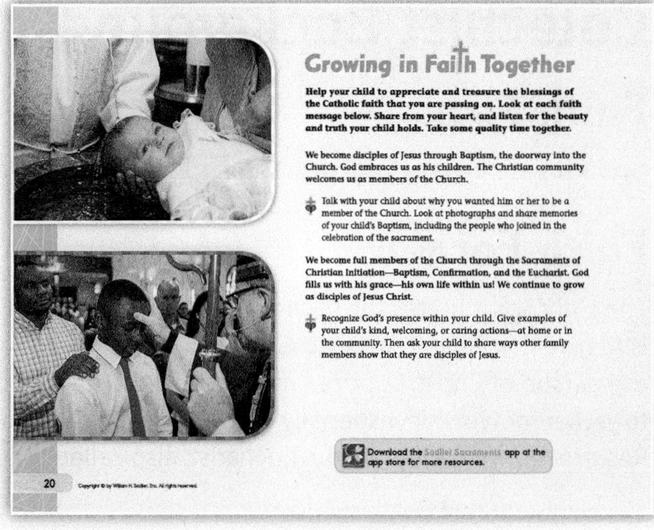

Growing in Faith Together

Help your child to appreciate and treasure the blessings of the Catholic faith that you are passing on. Look at each faith message below. Share from your heart, and listen for the beauty and truth your child holds. Take some quality time together.

We become disciples of Jesus through Baptism, the doorway into the Church. God embraces us as his children. The Christian community welcomes us as members of the Church.

- Talk with your child about why you wanted him or her to be a member of the Church. Look at photographs and share memories of your child's Baptism, including the people who joined in the celebration of the sacrament.

We become full members of the Church through the Sacraments of Christian Initiation—Baptism, Confirmation, and the Eucharist. God fills us with his grace—his own life within us! We continue to grow as disciples of Jesus Christ.

- Recognize God's presence within your child. Give examples of your child's kind, welcoming, or caring actions—at home or in the community. Then ask your child to share ways other family members show that they are disciples of Jesus.

Download the Sadlier Sacraments app at the app store for more resources.

20 Copyright © by William H. Sadlier, Inc. All rights reserved.

Celebrating Inclusion

Strategies and tips for including children with disabilities

Use the following tips to teach this chapter through a multisensory approach, which may benefit not only children with learning differences but others as well. The more we teach in a multisensory approach that includes auditory, visual, and tactile-kinesthetic (hands-on) opportunities for learning, the more learners we will reach when we teach.

Believe To complete page 8, small-group sharing can provide additional opportunities for auditory learning. Stop and think of ways you can intentionally include other sounds in a lesson. If a tactile-kinesthetic approach is best, you will want to incorporate movement into the activity. This could include the children acting their responses out.

Page 9 discusses "Doors that Welcome." Doors make sounds when opened and closed. Start this activity by gently opening and closing your room door. Hands-on learners would also love to open and close the room door; just remind them to do so gently.

On pages 10 and 11, make use of the beautiful illustration to engage visual learning. When using pictures, remember to always "read" the pictures to learners who have autism or Down syndrome, or anyone who is blind or visually impaired.

Celebrate For page 12, the instructions in the guide for using gestures to explain the word *Church* provide a good example of using movement to more fully engage the tactile-kinesthetic learner. Visual learners could be shown a diagram of increasingly larger circles of community, with family as the center, then parish, then diocese, and, finally, the worldwide Catholic Church.

For pages 12 through 15, consider letting the children "baptize" a baby doll using a bowl of water. Also engage visual learning through the photos. While the children are looking at a picture, describe it to them. For children who cannot respond verbally, instead of asking questions of them, tell them what you want them to know.

Live The use of music, both listening and participating, is also ideal. It will also be helpful to use simple pictures when giving directions, such as showing "prayer hands" when it's time to pray.

Gathering to Give Thanks and Praise

Catechist Background

Faith Focus

God's love is always with me, and I give thanks and praise!

Faith Formation

The Holy Spirit unites the Catholic Church in worship. To worship is to give thanks and praise to God. Led by the priest, acting in the person of Christ, baptized members of the Church gather together for worship, especially on the Lord's Day, the day of Jesus' Resurrection, to celebrate the Eucharist, also called the Mass.

The celebration of the Eucharist is the greatest prayer of the Church. The *Constitution on the Sacred Liturgy* says, "When the Church prays or sings or acts, the faith of those taking part is nourished and their minds are raised to God, so that they may . . . more abundantly receive His grace" (33). Jesus instituted the Eucharist at the Last Supper.

The Mass has these parts: the Introductory Rites, the Liturgy of the Word, the Liturgy of the Eucharist, and the Concluding Rites. The Introductory Rites prepare us to listen to the Word of God and to receive Holy Communion. During the Introductory Rites the Entrance Chant or song supports the unity of all gathered, introduces the liturgical season or feast, and accompanies the procession of the priest and other ministers. We make the Sign of the Cross as a sign that we gather in God's name. During the Penitential Act we praise God for his love and mercy. Except during the seasons of Advent and Lent, we sing or say the *Gloria*, a prayer of praise to God, the Father, Son, and Holy Spirit.

This chapter explores why we assemble on the Lord's Day and how we participate in this great prayer of thanksgiving and praise, the Eucharist, the center of Catholic life. The chapter focuses particularly on the Introductory Rites.

For Personal Reflection

Is my life centered on the celebration of the Eucharist? Do I actively participate in the Mass?

Catechist Prayer

Loving God, help the children to learn to center their lives on the celebration of the Eucharist. Hear their prayers as they gather around your altar. Nourish their minds, hearts, and souls.

Resources

Roman Missal

Constitution on the Sacred Liturgy (Sacrosanctum Concilium)

Catechism of the Catholic Church, 1156–1158, 1191, 1193, 1279, 1328, 1341, 1346, 1348, 2177

We Believe, Catholic Identity Edition, Grade 2, Chapter 16

Believe—Celebrate—Live: Eucharist DVD, Chapter 2 video; Music CD, "Rain Down."

Celebrating Inclusion

Strategies and tips for including children with disabilities are found on page 33–34.

Words of Faith

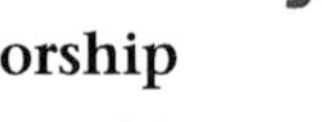

worship
assembly
vestments
Lord's Day
Introductory Rites

Introduce the Chapter

Review the lesson introduction on page 21.

Play the video segment introducing the chapter. Alternatively, share the story below.

Read-Aloud Story (Optional)

Megan

Last Sunday my brother, Connor, was an altar server at Mass. It was his first time serving.

When the music started, the assembly stood to sing. I saw Connor walking toward the altar. He looked different in his long white robe, called an alb. He was carrying a large crucifix. I wondered how heavy it was. Behind him were two other altar servers holding lighted candles. Deacon Tony and Father Marc were the last in the procession. They wore special vestments.

When Connor got to the altar, he bowed. The others in the procession bowed, too. Father Marc and Deacon Tony also kissed the altar. In my heart I knew God was with us.

The music stopped and it was quiet. Father Marc prayed, "In the name of the Father, and of the Son, and of the Holy Spirit." I made the Sign of the Cross and said, "Amen." I was ready to give thanks and praise to God!

- **How will I do this with my parish family?**

Gathering to Give Thanks and Praise

Chapter Planner

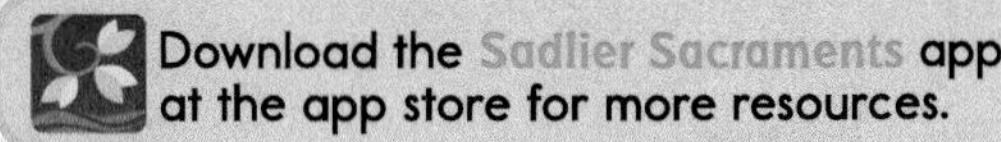

Time	Materials	Steps
Believe pages 21–25		
15–20 minutes	• battery-operated candle • Chapter 2 video • chart paper • Bible open to the Scripture passage on page 24, for direct reading of the Scripture	• Pray the words from the *Roman Missal*. • View and discuss the Chapter 2 video (or share the Read-Aloud Story, page 21B). • Complete the activity about meeting new people. • Read and discuss the text. • Discuss the photograph. • Complete the activity about working alone and with others. • Read aloud the Scripture story of Jesus' entry into Jerusalem for the Passover celebration, and engage in the *Lectio* and *Visio Divina* exercise.
Celebrate pages 26–29		
20–30 minutes	• drawing paper and crayons or colored pencils	• Present the text and complete the activities. • Present the "Catholic Identity" and "Catholic Faith and Life" features. • Discuss the photographs and captions. • Discuss the Words of Faith. • Present the "Celebrating Cultural Diversity" feature.
Live pages 30–32		
10–15 minutes	• prayer space materials listed on page 32 • *Believe—Celebrate—Live* Music CD	• Prepare the prayer space. • Discuss ways we give thanks and praise. • Complete the activity. • Read and respond to the "Discipleship in Action" story and activity. • Pray and sing "Rain Down Your Love." • Close with reflection questions. • Remind the children to bring home the "Living Faith at Home" page.

Key: Prayer Video Scripture 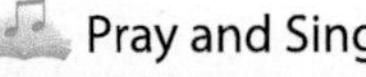 Pray and Sing

Introduce the Chapter

Gathering to Give Thanks and Praise

Welcome the children and tell them that they will take a closer look at how the Catholic Church gathers to worship God.

Gather for prayer. Light a battery-operated candle. Invite the children to look around to see who is present. Remind them that God is always present when they gather together to pray. Pray together the Sign of the Cross. Greet the children by saying, "May God be with each one of you." Invite the children to pray the response "And with your spirit" on page 21.

Explain that this is our response at Mass after the priest's greeting, "The Lord be with you." At Mass, the priest is expressing his desire that the action and presence of God's Spirit will be with the Church, the People of God. The response "And with your spirit" is only for an ordained minister, a priest or deacon. It acknowledges the Holy Spirit given to these men at ordination in the hope that they will use their gifts in their ministry to the Church.

Direct attention to the photograph on this page.

Ask *How is this family enjoying God's gifts?*

Share with the children that we gather with our parish family for the celebration of the Eucharist, or the Mass, to praise God and thank him for all that he gives us. The word *eucharist* means "thanksgiving."

Introduce the video segment for this chapter by saying, "Let's explore some of the themes of this chapter with our young friends from the chapter video." Play the video.

Alternatively, you may choose to share the Read-Aloud Story found on page 21B of this guide.

Notes ______________________________

____

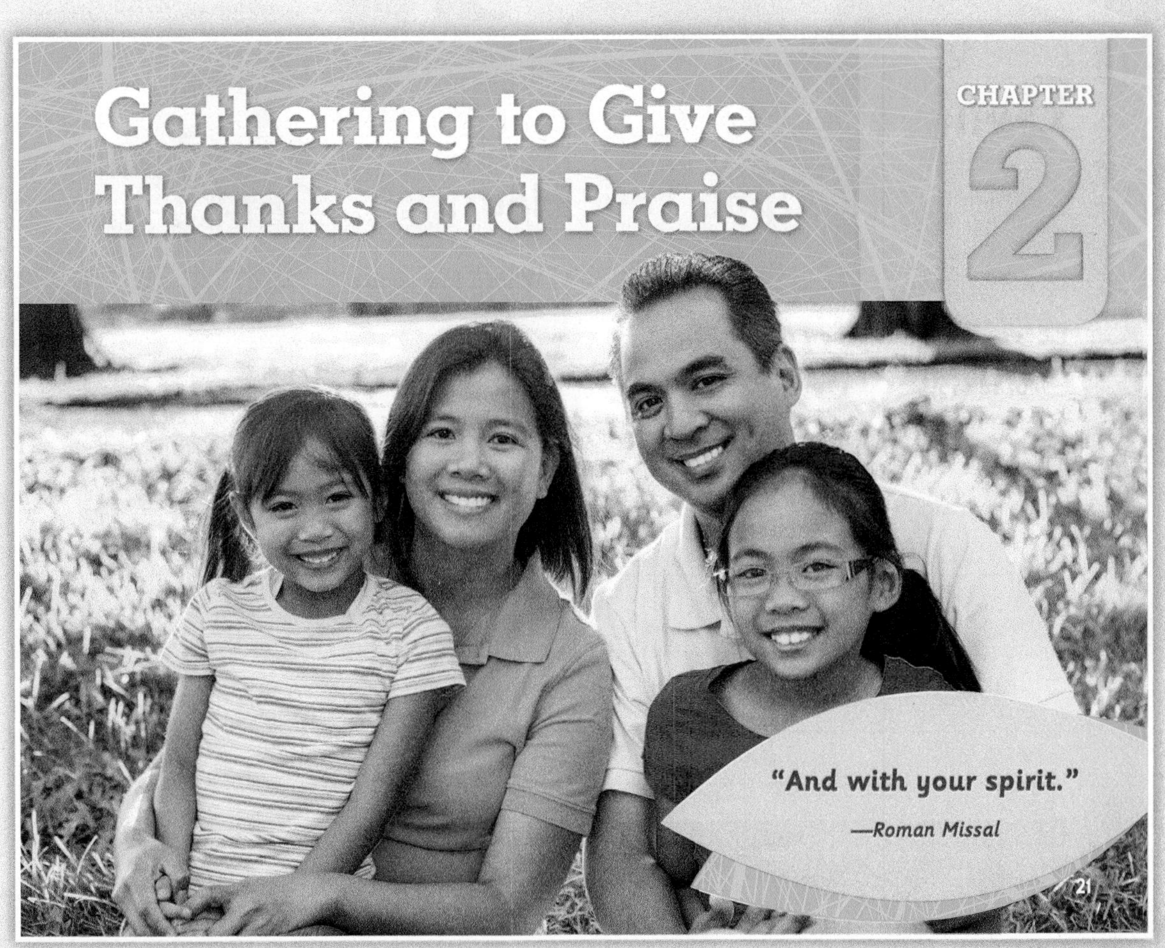
Gathering to Give
Thanks and Praise
CHAPTER
2
"And with your spirit."
—Roman Missal
21

Believe

Open Your Heart

Ask the children the following or similar questions about what they saw in the video or heard in the Read-Aloud Story:

Why does the Catholic family gather on Sundays or Saturday evening?

What did you see or hear that reminds you of how your parish family celebrates Mass?

What is your favorite part of Mass?

Explain "When you go to Mass, you may see friends and families that you know. There may also be people who are new to you."

Activity

- Invite the children to complete the sections "Places where I meet new people" and "What I like about being with others." Invite volunteers to share their responses.
- Share with the children your own experiences of meeting new people and ways they have worked together with you.
- Invite the children to complete "Ways new friends help me." Talk about how new friends count on them as well. Ask: *What are some ways that you help your new friends?*

Notes ______

______

______

______

Believe

Open Your Heart

What I like about being with others:

______

______

______

______

Places where I meet new people:

☐ at school

☐ at family gatherings

☐ in my neighborhood

other: ______

______

______

______

______

Ways new friends help me:

______

______

______

______

22

Connecting with Others

Direct attention to the picture of the children forming a human bridge. Explain that this image reminds us that we are all connected to one another. Every day we do things with others.

Read the first paragraph.

Ask *How do you feel when you make a new friend? What is the difference between doing things alone and doing things with others?*

Read the Scripture quote from the Gospel of Matthew together. Ask the children who they think is speaking. Explain that God is with us when we gather as a community to pray.

Read the last paragraph.

Ask *How are we connected to the people in our parish family? What do we share together?*

Activity

- Invite the children to think about ways they spend time with others each day. Recall the activity they completed about making new friends and ways they work together.
- List the following activities on chart paper: eat a meal, play a game, do homework, tell a story, paint a picture. Have the children tell which activities they can do alone and which they usually share with others. Explain that there are many ways that we are connected to others.

Notes ______________________

____

____

____

Connecting with Others

Each of us is connected to other people. At school, for example, we gather with other children to learn, share ideas, and make new friends.

How do you feel when you make a new friend? What is the difference between doing things alone and doing things with others?

Through the grace of our Baptism we are connected to Jesus and his Church. When we gather with our parish community at Mass, we share and celebrate our love for God. By the power of the Holy Spirit, Jesus is with the Church as we remember him and give praise and thanks to God.

"Where two or three are gathered together in my name, there am I in the midst of them."

MATTHEW 18:20

Believe

The Word of the Lord

Share that Jerusalem was a very important city to the Jewish People because the Temple was there. On some of their feasts the Jewish People would travel to Jerusalem and gather in the Temple to celebrate.

Read aloud the introductory paragraph before the Scripture.

Explain that the Church remembers this event from Scripture at the beginning of Holy Week, on Palm Sunday, the Sunday before Easter. We also have a special procession, a prayerful walk together, during which we carry palm branches and sing songs of praise.

Guide the children through an adaptation of *Lectio Divina*, a special way to pray with Scripture. Quiet the children, and ask them to listen carefully to the Scripture reading as you read it aloud.

Reflect on the reading by inviting the children to:

- Take a moment to think about what they heard.
- Silently answer the following questions for reflection (be sure to pause after each question): *What word or words did you hear? What do you think Jesus is saying to you?*
- Quietly hold these words in their hearts. (Pause in prayer.)
- Share aloud in one or two words what they heard. Describe what they were feeling in their hearts. (Accept all responses.)

Guide the children through an adaptation of *Visio Divina*, a special way to pray with Scripture art. Quiet the children, and invite them to take their time looking at the illustration on pages 24 and 25. Read aloud the Scripture once again. Invite the children to silently answer these questions: *What do you see? What does it mean to you? What do you imagine Jesus inviting you to see? What do you think this means for you?*

Believe

The Word of the Lord

Jesus and his disciples often gathered together to celebrate Jewish feasts and holy days. Together they gave praise and thanks to God the Father for his blessings. For some feasts they went to the Temple in Jerusalem to celebrate with other Jewish families. The Temple was the holy place where Jewish People prayed and worshiped God.

Based on MARK 11:8–9

The week before Jesus died and rose again, he and his disciples went to Jerusalem. Many people were there to celebrate the important Jewish feast of Passover. People heard that Jesus and his disciples were coming to celebrate. Many people went to meet Jesus. Some spread out their coats on the road. Others spread palm tree branches or waved them as Jesus passed. People began to praise Jesus. They called out,

"Hosanna!
Blessed is he who comes in the name of the Lord!"

(Mark 11:9)

24

Share After the silent reflection, allow time for sharing aloud responses to these questions. Then invite the children to look again at the picture and silently answer the questions: *What are some things this picture tells you about showing love for Jesus Christ? How can we be welcoming to Jesus?* Invite volunteers to share their responses aloud.

Check comprehension by asking the following questions:
What did the people do to welcome Jesus to Jerusalem? (They spread out their coats on the road. They spread tree branches on the road, or they waved the branches in the air as Jesus passed by them. This action is similar to our "rolling out the red carpet" for someone very important.)
What did the people say to welcome Jesus to Jerusalem? (They called out:
"Hosanna!
Blessed is he who comes in the name of
the Lord!" (Mark 11:9)

These are words of praise. Point out that we pray these words at Mass during the Liturgy of the Eucharist, when we pray the "Holy, Holy, Holy.")

Scripture Background

Passover is a very important feast for the Jewish People. During this eight-day feast they remember their escape from the ruler of Egypt who had kept them in slavery. In Jesus' time many people traveled to Jerusalem to celebrate the feast of Passover. They gathered in the Temple to worship God.

Notes ______________________

____

____

____

Celebrate

Gathered for Worship

Direct attention to the photo on the page. Ask: *What do you think these families are doing?* Guide the children to conclude that they are gathering for Mass on Sunday.

Ask *Who do you think is inside the church building preparing for the celebration of the Mass?* (priests, deacons, altar servers, and other ministers) Explain that when the people enter the church building, and Mass begins, a priest will lead the parish community in the celebration of the Eucharist.

Read aloud the first paragraph on this page. Explain why we gather for Mass and what the roles of the assembly, priest, and deacon are.

Ask *What does it mean to worship God?* (to praise and thank him) Stress that the celebration of the Eucharist is also called the Mass. The Mass is the greatest prayer of thanksgiving of the Church.

Invite the children to listen carefully to learn why Sunday is so important to Catholics.

Read aloud the final paragraph on page 26. Ask: *Why do we celebrate Mass on a Sunday?* (It is the day Jesus rose from the dead.)

Activity

- Distribute drawing materials (paper and crayons or colored pencils).
- Ask the children to write the word *Sunday* in the center of the paper. Invite them to draw pictures of their family celebrating the Lord's Day.
- Invite the children to share their drawings.

Celebrate

Gathered for Worship

People of all ages and backgrounds gather for Mass to worship God.

Every Sunday we gather with our parish to worship God as our Creator and Lord. To **worship** God means to "praise and thank" him. We do this in the greatest prayer of thanksgiving, which we call the Eucharist. This celebration of the Eucharist is also called the Mass. By special words and actions, we show that we believe that God is with us. Most of all, we remember and celebrate how Jesus saved us by his suffering, Death, Resurrection, and Ascension. The community of people who gather for the celebration of the Eucharist is called the **assembly**. Our parish priest leads the assembly in this celebration. He is called the celebrant. A deacon often assists him. At Mass the priest and the deacon wear special clothing called **vestments**.

It was on a Sunday that Jesus Christ rose from the dead to new life. So, Sunday is the most special day for the Church. On Sunday we worship with our parish community, rest from work, and take time to be with our family.

Read aloud the first paragraph on page 27. Share the Holy Days of Obligation: Solemnity of Mary, the Holy Mother of God, January 1; Ascension of the Lord, when celebrated on Thursday forty days after Easter Sunday; Assumption of the Blessed Virgin Mary, August 15; All Saints, November 1; Immaculate Conception of the Blessed Virgin Mary, December 8; Nativity of the Lord (Christmas), December 25.

Read aloud the last two paragraphs. Reiterate that during Mass we remember Jesus' life, Death, Resurrection, and Ascension. Explain Jesus' Ascension by saying that Jesus stayed with his disciples for forty days after his Resurrection. When it was time for him to return to his Father, he ascended into heaven.

Catholic Faith and Life

Read the feature on the Sacrament of Holy Orders. Stress that priests act in the person of Christ in celebrating Mass and the other sacraments. "Christ himself, the eternal high priest of the New Covenant, acting through the ministry of the priests, offers the Eucharistic sacrifice." (*CCC*, 1410)

Words of Faith

worship (page 26)
assembly (page 26)
vestments (page 26)
Lord's Day (page 27)

Celebrating Cultural Diversity

Traditions and customs from cultures that make up our one Church

Different cultures may incorporate their musical traditions and customs into their celebration of the Eucharist. For example, in Kenya, a country in East Africa, the musical instruments used to play sacred music may be made locally, and include drums, flutes, shakers, and xylophones. The sacred songs may be sung in Swahili or another local language, and may include dance movements and gestures. Diversity in sacred music reinforces our Catholic Identity.

The Church tells us to worship God by taking part in the Mass every Sunday of the year. We are also to attend Mass on other special days called Holy Days of Obligation. When we do this, we follow the Third Commandment and one of the laws of the Church.

Through the Sacrament of Holy Orders, a man is ordained a priest. Many priests serve in local parishes. They spend their lives sharing God's love with people. They act in the person of Christ in celebrating Mass and the other sacraments.

Sunday is called the **Lord's Day**. Its celebration lasts from Saturday evening through Sunday until midnight. We gather with our parish to celebrate the Mass on this day because it is the day Jesus rose from the dead. We celebrate the salvation that Jesus made possible by his sacrifice on the Cross. He fills us, the Body of Christ, with the grace of his salvation. The celebration of the Eucharist is the center of the Church's life.

In the celebration of the Eucharist, the Mass, we show God our love by singing, praying, and listening to the Word of God. Together, with the priest, we

- praise and thank God
- listen to the Word of God
- remember Jesus' life, Death, Resurrection, and Ascension
- receive Jesus in Holy Communion.

Celebrate

The Introductory Rites

Direct attention to the photograph on page 28. Explain that at the beginning of Mass there is a procession to the altar. The procession creates a sacred atmosphere, unites us, and gathers us into a holy assembly. The procession is led by the altar servers, who carry the cross and candles. Other ministers may follow. The deacon, if present, follows and carries the Book of the Gospels, which is placed on the altar. The priest then follows.

Direct attention to the "Eucharist: Parish Church Tour" feature on pages 4 and 5 of the child's book. Explain that when the altar servers reach the sanctuary, they may place the candles on or alongside the altar, one at each end. When the priest and the deacon reach the altar, they kiss the altar. The altar server may place the crucifix in a stand behind or near the altar. Explain that there are four parts of the Mass: the Introductory Rites, the Liturgy of the Word, the Liturgy of the Eucharist, and the Concluding Rites.

Read aloud the first paragraph on page 28. Then ask: *What do the Introductory Rites help us to do?* (The Introductory Rites help us to remember that we are a worshiping community. They prepare us to listen to the Word of God and celebrate the Eucharist.)

Explain that the two main parts of the Mass are the Liturgy of the Word and the Liturgy of the Eucharist. The prayers of the Introductory Rites prepare us for the two main parts of the celebration.

Read aloud the remaining text on page 28.

Activity

Have the children act out the words and actions of the priest and the assembly as described in the Introductory Rites. The prayers can be found in missalettes or hymnals.

Celebrate

We begin the Mass by praying through song. This song introduces the liturgical season and feast and expresses our unity.

The Introductory Rites

The Mass begins with the **Introductory Rites**. These prayers and actions help us to remember that we are a worshiping community. They prepare us to listen to the Word of God and celebrate the Eucharist. In the Introductory Rites:

- We stand and sing to express our unity as the baptized. As the assembly sings, the priest, deacon, and other ministers process to the altar.
- Those in the procession bow to the altar or genuflect to the tabernacle, and the priest and deacon kiss the altar as a sign of reverence for the Lord's Table.
- We make the Sign of the Cross. Then the priest greets us. His words and our response remind us that we gather in God's name.
- The priest asks us to silently think about our sins, the times we have not loved God and others.

Read aloud the first bulleted text on page 29. Explain that when we ask God for mercy, we are acknowledging our sins and praising God for his love and forgiveness. Read the "Lord, have mercy" prayer together. Explain that sometimes at Mass we sing this prayer.

Read aloud the second bulleted text, about the *Gloria*, our prayer of praise. If time allows, stand and pray these words now. You may want to explain that this prayer is not prayed during the liturgical seasons of Advent or Lent because of the emphasis on penance during these seasons.

Direct attention to the photograph on this page. Explain that the priest is praying the opening prayer, to which we respond, "Amen." Review the Introductory Rites by asking for a description of what is shown in each photograph on pages 28 and 29.

Share the importance of each person's participation during the Introductory Rites.

Explain that we stand during this part of the Mass. It is very important to understand that "music is . . . a sign of God's love for us" (*Sing to the Lord: Music in Divine Worship*, 2). We show God our love by joining others in song and prayer.

Words of Faith

Introductory Rites (page 28)

CATHOLIC IDENTITY

Read the statement together. Pray together: *Loving God, you have given us many blessings. We praise you and give you thanks.*

Notes ______________________________

____

____

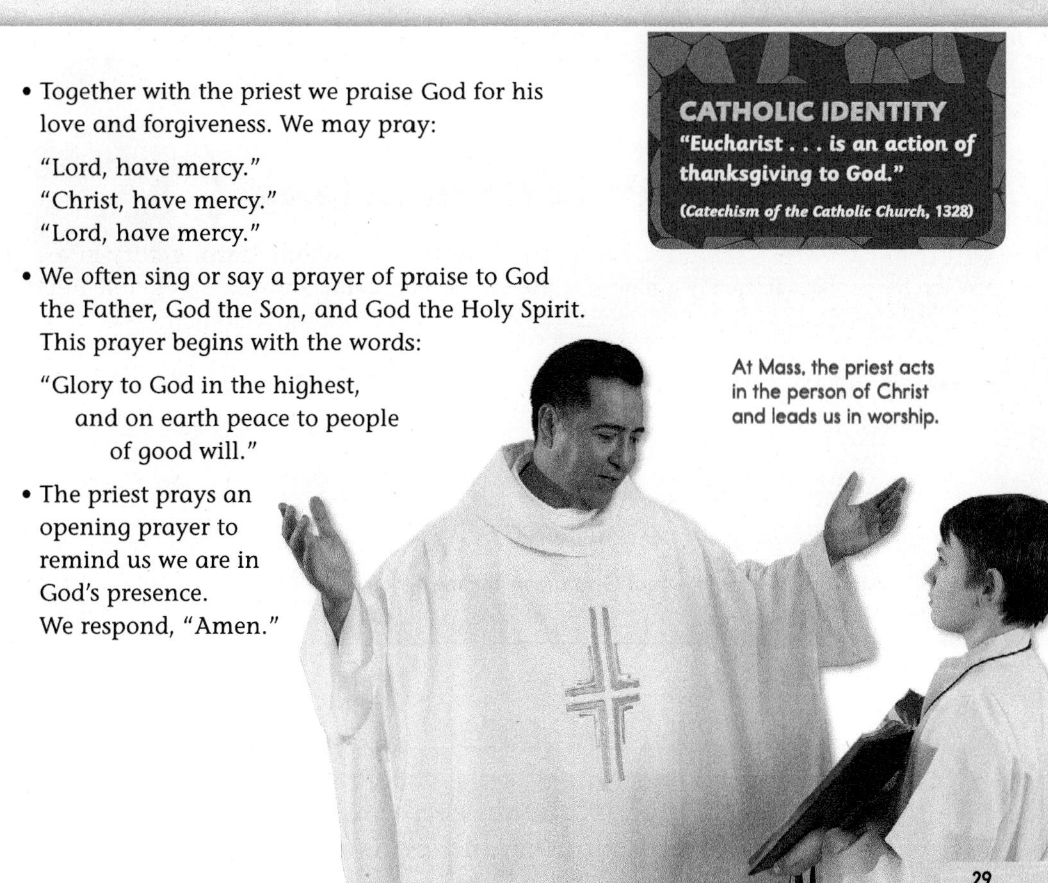

• Together with the priest we praise God for his love and forgiveness. We may pray:
"Lord, have mercy."
"Christ, have mercy."
"Lord, have mercy."
• We often sing or say a prayer of praise to God the Father, God the Son, and God the Holy Spirit. This prayer begins with the words:
"Glory to God in the highest, and on earth peace to people of good will."
• The priest prays an opening prayer to remind us we are in God's presence. We respond, "Amen."
CATHOLIC IDENTITY
"Eucharist . . . is an action of thanksgiving to God."
(Catechism of the Catholic Church, 1328)
At Mass, the priest acts in the person of Christ and leads us in worship.
29

Live

Become What You Believe

Invite the children to remember that the Mass is the greatest prayer of the Church. At Mass we pray with words, songs, and special movements and actions. All are ways that we, the worshiping community, give thanks and praise to God.

Notes ____________________

____

____

____

____

____

Activity

- Read aloud the first three sentence starters.
- Invite the children to imagine they are with their parish family now for the celebration of Mass. Ask them to think about what the priest and the assembly are doing and saying: *What is happening on the altar? in the pews?* Have the children complete the sentences and share their responses with a partner.
- Recall with the children the prayers and actions of the Mass that they learned about in this chapter. Invite them to complete the last sentence starter: *At Mass I especially feel God's love for me when . . .*

Live

Become What You Believe

When my parish community gathers for the celebration of the Mass:

I see . . .

I hear . . .

I pray . . .

At Mass I especially feel God's love for me when . . .

God's love is always with me, and I give thanks and praise.

30

Discipleship in Action

Read aloud the story of Saint Maria Guadalupe on page 31. Explain that Maria loved God, and she cared about the people in her community. She prayed for them, and she worked with others to help them.

Invite the children to share ways Saint Maria Guadalupe helped her community. Talk about people in their own communities who need help, such as people who have lost their jobs or their homes, or families who are caring for someone who is very sick.

Activity

Encourage the children to draw a picture of people in their community who need their help. Then have them write one way they will help these people and one way they will keep the people in their prayers.

Notes

Discipleship in Action

Saint Maria Guadalupe (1878–1963)

Saint Maria Guadalupe was born in Mexico. From an early age, she tried to live as a good disciple of Jesus. She prayed often. She was devoted to the Blessed Virgin Mary. Maria also wanted to help people in her community. When she grew up, she decided not to get married. Instead, she became a religious sister to help people in need. Maria founded a new congregation of sisters who served the community. Maria raised money to support the community's hospital. Today the congregation that Maria started serves many poor and sick people in the community.

Here is a drawing of people in the community I can help:

Here is one way I might help them:

Here is a way I will pray for them:

Live 

Rain Down Your Love 

Read and familiarize yourself with the prayer and the music selection. To prepare the environment, arrange the following items on a small table:

- white tablecloth
- baptismal candle in holder
- small cross that can be passed around
- Bible on a table stand

You will also need:

- CD player
- Music CD, queued to play the track "Rain Down"

Invite the children to gather around the table with their books. Teach them the song "Rain Down." Ask the children to quiet themselves for prayer. Point to the part of the prayer where they will be passing a cross to each other. Explain that while they are holding the cross, they may say a silent prayer. (Instrumental music will be playing.) Pray the prayer together, ending with the Lord's Prayer (page 93 of child's book).

Conclude the prayer ritual with the following "mystagogy," or reflection on the experience. Invite the children to give one- or two-word responses to the following:

- *How did it feel to receive the cross and pray?*
- *What does "rain down your love" mean to you?*
- *How does God speak to us?*
- *Why do we ask God to rain down his love and mercy?*

Notes ______________________________

____

____

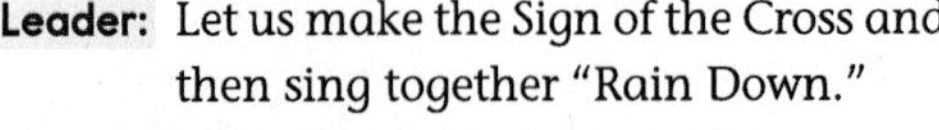

Rain Down Your Love 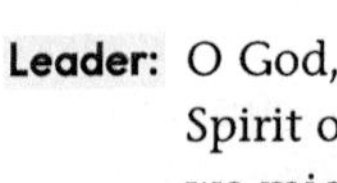

Leader: Let us make the Sign of the Cross and then sing together "Rain Down."

All: (*Refrain*) Rain down, rain down, rain down your love on your people. Rain down, rain down, rain down your love, God of life.

Leader: God of all creation, we believe that you rain down your love on the earth. Fill us with your mercy as we turn our hearts to you in prayer.

All: (*Sing refrain.*)

Leader: Loving and merciful God, we thank you for the gift of your Son, Jesus. With great joy in our hearts, we give thanks and celebrate with all of our brothers and sisters.

All: (*Sing refrain.*)

Leader: O God, you rain down your Holy Spirit on all who follow you, that we might be your eyes, your hands, and your feet in this world. Thank you for filling us with your love.

All: (*Sing refrain.*)

Leader: We ask God to bless us and those we love, and to help us to remember how much Jesus loves us.

Leader: I invite you take hold of the cross, say a prayer, and then pass the cross on. (*instrumental music*)

All: (*Sing refrain.*)

Leader: Let us join hands and pray as Jesus taught us.

All: Our Father . . .

32

Living Faith at Home

Encourage family participation by having the children take home the double-sided "Living Faith at Home" page.

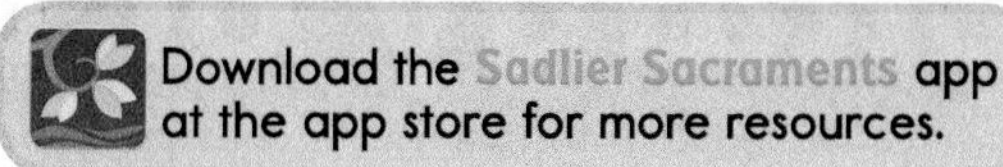

Living Faith at Home

"Hosanna! Blessed is he who comes in the name of the Lord!"

MARK 11:9

Take a few minutes to reflect on the Scripture art. Ask God to open your eyes and your heart. What feelings are you experiencing? How do you welcome and honor Jesus with your parish community? Pray a silent prayer of gratitude.

33

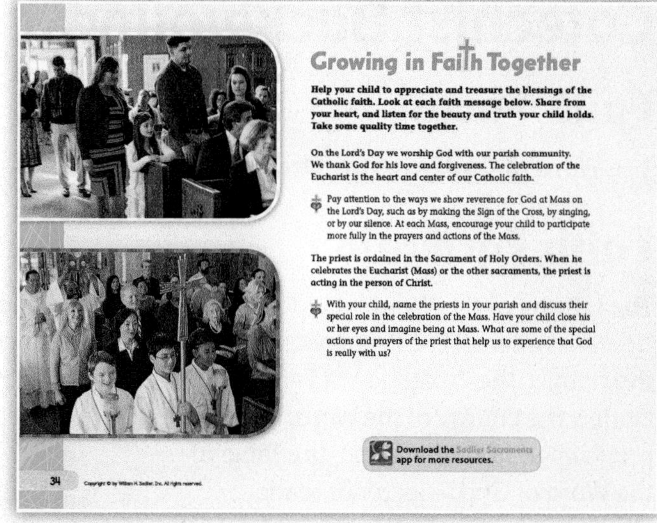

Growing in Faith Together

Help your child to appreciate and treasure the blessings of the Catholic faith. Look at each faith message below. Share from your heart, and listen for the beauty and truth your child holds. Take some quality time together.

On the Lord's Day we worship God with our parish community. We thank God for his love and forgiveness. The celebration of the Eucharist is the heart and center of our Catholic faith.

Pay attention to the ways we show reverence for God at Mass on the Lord's Day, such as by making the Sign of the Cross, by singing, or by our silence. At each Mass, encourage your child to participate more fully in the prayers and actions of the Mass.

The priest is ordained in the Sacrament of Holy Orders. When he celebrates the Eucharist (Mass) or the other sacraments, the priest is acting in the person of Christ.

With your child, name the priests in your parish and discuss their special role in the celebration of the Mass. Have your child close his or her eyes and imagine being at Mass. What are some of the special actions and prayers of the priest that help us to experience that God is really with us?

Download the Sadlier Sacraments app for more resources.

34

Celebrating Inclusion

Strategies and tips for including children with disabilities

Use the following tips to teach this chapter through a multisensory approach, which may benefit not only children with learning differences but others as well. The more we teach in a multisensory approach that includes auditory, visual, and tactile-kinesthetic (hands-on) opportunities for learning, the more learners we will reach when we teach.

Believe On page 22, to help auditory learners, have the children share responses with a partner.

For page 23, hands-on learners will enjoy forming a human bridge as shown in the photo on this page. Allow children who are uncomfortable with physical touch to draw a picture of other children holding hands or to connect with other children by holding onto the same scarf or rope.

Hands-on learners will enjoy role-play based on the Scripture account on page 24. Use strips of green construction paper for palm branches, and invite the children to wave their branches while saying, "Hosanna! / Blessed is he who comes in the name of the Lord!"

Celebrate For page 26, show visual learners pictures that depict activities at Mass, such as the priest at the altar or people processing to receive the Eucharist. Play "Simon Says" using gestures of the assembly at Mass, such as standing, sitting, kneeling, or bowing, to engage tactile-kinesthetic learners.

For page 27, when teaching about the Sacrament of Holy Orders, invite the pastor or parish priest to visit the class and offer a blessing. This will be especially helpful for visual and tactile-kinesthetic learners.

For page 28, tactile-kinesthetic learners will benefit from standing to sing a song as well as practicing the Sign of the Cross for the Introductory Rites.

Live Allow children who have difficulty writing to respond verbally to pages 30 and 31. For children with intellectual or developmental delays, share photos of things that can be seen, heard, or prayed at Mass for page 30.

On page 32, teach the following movements for the refrain: For "Rain down," raise hands, then lower them while wiggling fingers (three times); for "your love," form a heart shape by cupping hands over head; and for "on your people," open arms wide.

Celebrating the Liturgy of the Word

Catechist Background

Faith Focus

The Word of God gives me strength.

Faith Formation

The Liturgy of the Word includes readings from the Old and the New Testaments, the Responsorial Psalm, the Gospel Acclamation, the homily, the Profession of Faith, and the Prayer of the Faithful. During the Liturgy of the Word, readings from Scripture are proclaimed from the ambo, the Table of the Word of God. A lector or reader proclaims the First and Second Readings from the Lectionary. A cantor or psalmist leads the Responsorial Psalm after the First Reading. The Gospel, which is the high point of the Liturgy of the Word, is read from the *Book of the Gospels* by the priest or deacon.

In the Scripture readings, God speaks to us, here and now. We listen and learn of God's love and mercy, his work of salvation. "When the Sacred Scriptures are read in the Church, God himself speaks to his people, and Christ, present in his word, proclaims the Gospel." (*General Instruction of the Roman Missal*, 29)

Sacred Scripture strengthens our faith, renews our hope, and moves us to charity. "The force and power in the word of God is so great that it stands as the support and energy of the Church, the strength of faith for her sons, the food of the soul, the pure and everlasting source of spiritual life." *(Dogmatic Constitution on Divine Revelation*, 21)

Help the children to appreciate Scripture as the Word of God. Show them a Bible, and explain that we hear readings from the Bible at every Mass from a special collection of Scripture passages called the Lectionary. Through Scripture God reveals himself and his loving plan for all creation. Encourage the children to keep the Word of God in their hearts and allow it to guide their lives.

For Personal Reflection

Do I listen to the Word of God with reverence, believing that it is God himself who is speaking to me? How do I respond to the Word of God and apply it in my life?

Catechist Prayer

Holy Spirit, enlighten the minds of the children and fill their hearts with love as they listen to Sacred Scripture. Help them to live according to the Word of God.

Resources

General Instruction of the Roman Missal

Catechism of the Catholic Church, 197, 1088, 1100–1102, 1171, 1190, 1194, 1349, 1345–1355, 1408

We Believe, Catholic Identity Edition, Grade 2, Chapter 17

Believe—Celebrate—Live: Eucharist DVD, Chapter 3 video; Music CD, "Lord, Hear My Prayer"

Celebrating Inclusion

Strategies and tips for including children with disabilities are found on page 47–48.

Words of Faith

Liturgy of the Word
psalm
Gospel
homily
Creed
Prayer of the Faithful
lector
Lectionary
ambo
Book of the Gospels

Introduce the Chapter

Review the lesson introduction on page 35.

Play the video segment introducing the chapter. Alternatively, share the story below.

Read-Aloud Story (Optional)

James

The name of my pastor is Father Andrew. At Mass he gets to read from the *Book of the Gospels*. Only a priest or deacon can do this at the celebration of the Eucharist.

At Mass, Father Andrew holds the book up high, and he traces the Sign of the Cross on the book. That's how I know that this is not an ordinary book because the Gospel is the Word of God. My parish family knows this, too. Together we stand and sing the Gospel Acclamation!

Then Father Andrew says, "A reading from the holy Gospel. . . ." With the rest of my parish family I pray, "Glory to you, O Lord."

I stand with the assembly as I listen to the reading from the Gospel. I try to picture myself being in the stories. They take place at the top of mountains, along roads, and even in people's homes. Sometimes Jesus reminds me to share with others. In some Gospels, Jesus asks me to be more forgiving. In all the Gospels, I feel Jesus' love for me.

I am glad Jesus is with me!

- **What should I do after I listen to the Gospel?**

Celebrating the Liturgy of the Word

Chapter Planner

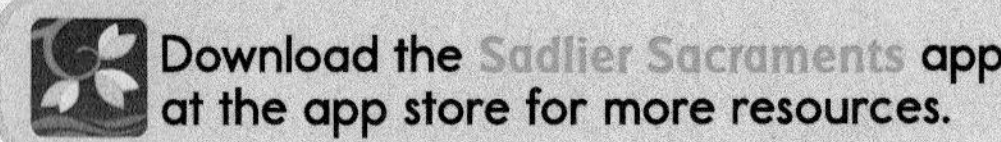
Download the Sadlier Sacraments app at the app store for more resources.

Time	Materials	Steps
Believe pages 35–39		
15–20 minutes	• battery-operated candle • Chapter 3 video • drawing paper and crayons • Bible open to the Scripture passage on page 38, for direct reading of the Scripture	• Pray the words from the *Roman Missal*. • View and discuss the Chapter 3 video (or share the Read-Aloud Story, page 35B) • Read and discuss the text. • Discuss the photograph. • Complete the drawing activity on listening to God's message. • Read aloud the Scripture story of the Parable of the Sower, and engage in the *Lectio* and *Visio Divina* exercise.
Celebrate pages 40–43		
20–30 minutes	• chart paper or board • paper cut-out circles, two per child	• Present the text and complete the activities. • Present the "Catholic Identity" and "Catholic Faith and Life" features. • Discuss the photographs and captions. • Discuss the Words of Faith. • Present the "Celebrating Cultural Diversity" feature.
Live pages 44–46		
10–15 minutes	• prayer space materials listed on page 46 • *Believe—Celebrate—Live* Music CD	• Prepare the prayer space. • Discuss ways the Word of God gives us strength. • Complete the activity. • Read and respond to the "Discipleship in Action" story and activity. • Pray and sing "Lord, Hear My Prayer/*Oyenos, Señor*" • Close with reflection questions. • Remind the children to bring home the "Living Faith at Home" page.

Key: Prayer · Video · Scripture · Pray and Sing

Introduce the Chapter

Celebrating the Liturgy of the Word

Welcome the children and tell them that they will be learning more about ways we listen to God.

Gather for prayer in a space where you can display an open Bible or Lectionary. Light a battery-operated candle. Then pray together the Sign of the Cross. Call attention to the prayer of praise on page 35, from the *Roman Missal*. Together, praise God with these words. Then, invite the children to pray the response a second time, this time singing it to a simple tune.

Explain that this response is prayed aloud by the assembly before the priest or deacon reads the Gospel.

Direct attention to the photograph on this page. Talk about how families enjoy spending time together. Explain that listening to important words spoken by others and sharing important thoughts and feelings with others are two ways in which families grow together in love.

Introduce the video segment for this chapter by saying, "Let's explore some of the themes of this chapter with our young friends from the chapter video." Play the video.

Alternatively, you may choose to share the Read-Aloud Story found on page 35B of this guide.

Notes ______________________________

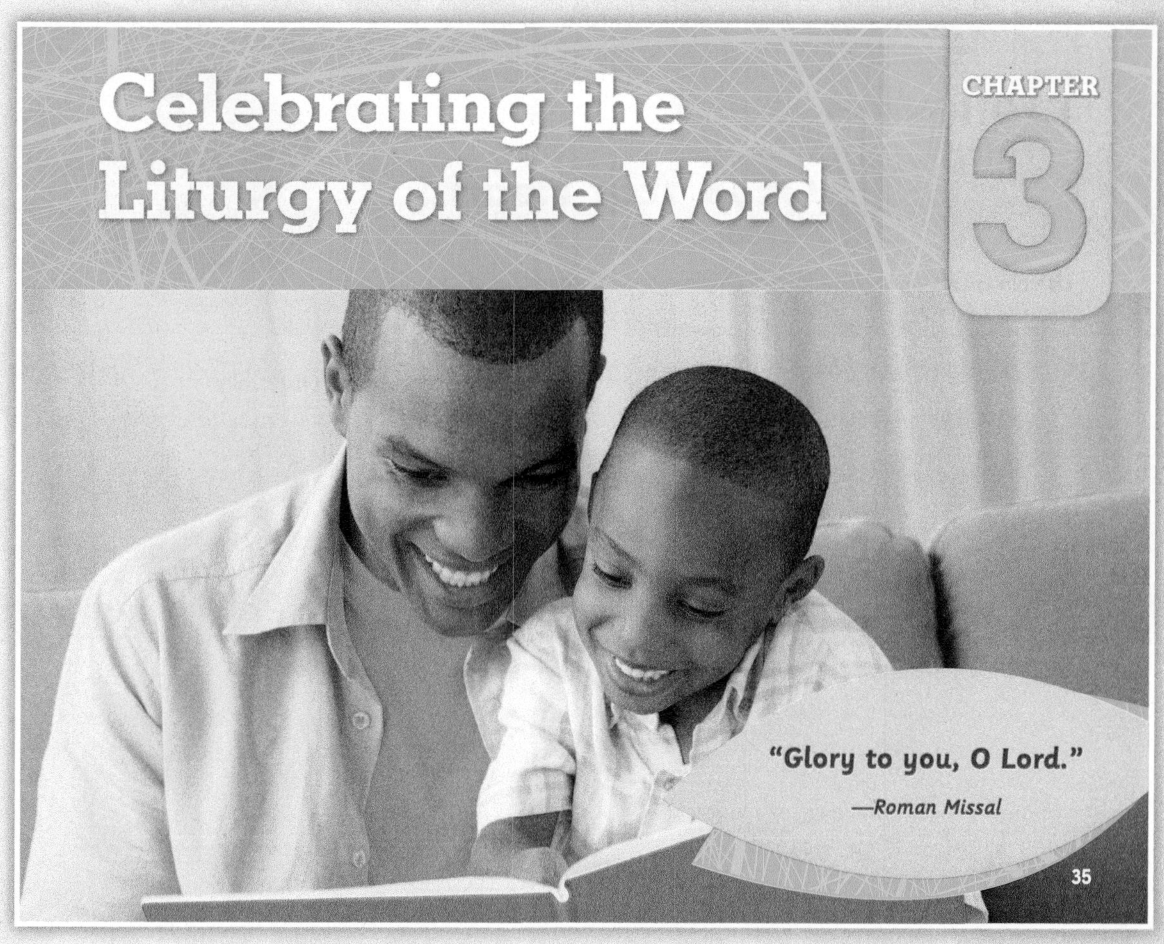
Celebrating the Liturgy of the Word
CHAPTER
3
"Glory to you, O Lord."
—Roman Missal
35

Believe

Open Your Heart

Ask the children the following or similar questions about what they saw in the video or heard in the Read-Aloud Story:

What is the Word of God?

Why do we listen to the Word of God at Mass?
Note: Emphasize to the children that we should listen attentively during the proclamation of Scripture at Mass.

What did you see or hear that was different or new to you?

Explain "It is God himself who is speaking to us when we listen to the proclamation of the Word of God."

Activity

Invite the children to tell about their experiences listening to others by completing the sentences.

People I like to listen to include . . .
Have the children draw or list friends, family members, teachers, or other adults they find interesting to listen to. Talk about why they like listening to these people.

Places where I listen to others include . . .
Brainstorm with the children the types of things we listen to, such as conversations or stories. Then invite the children to name some of the places where they would listen to others.

A picture of me listening carefully to someone . . .
Have children demonstrate what a good listener looks like. They may wish to sit up straighter or change the expression on their faces. Invite them to draw a picture of themselves with someone they like to listen to. Invite sharing.

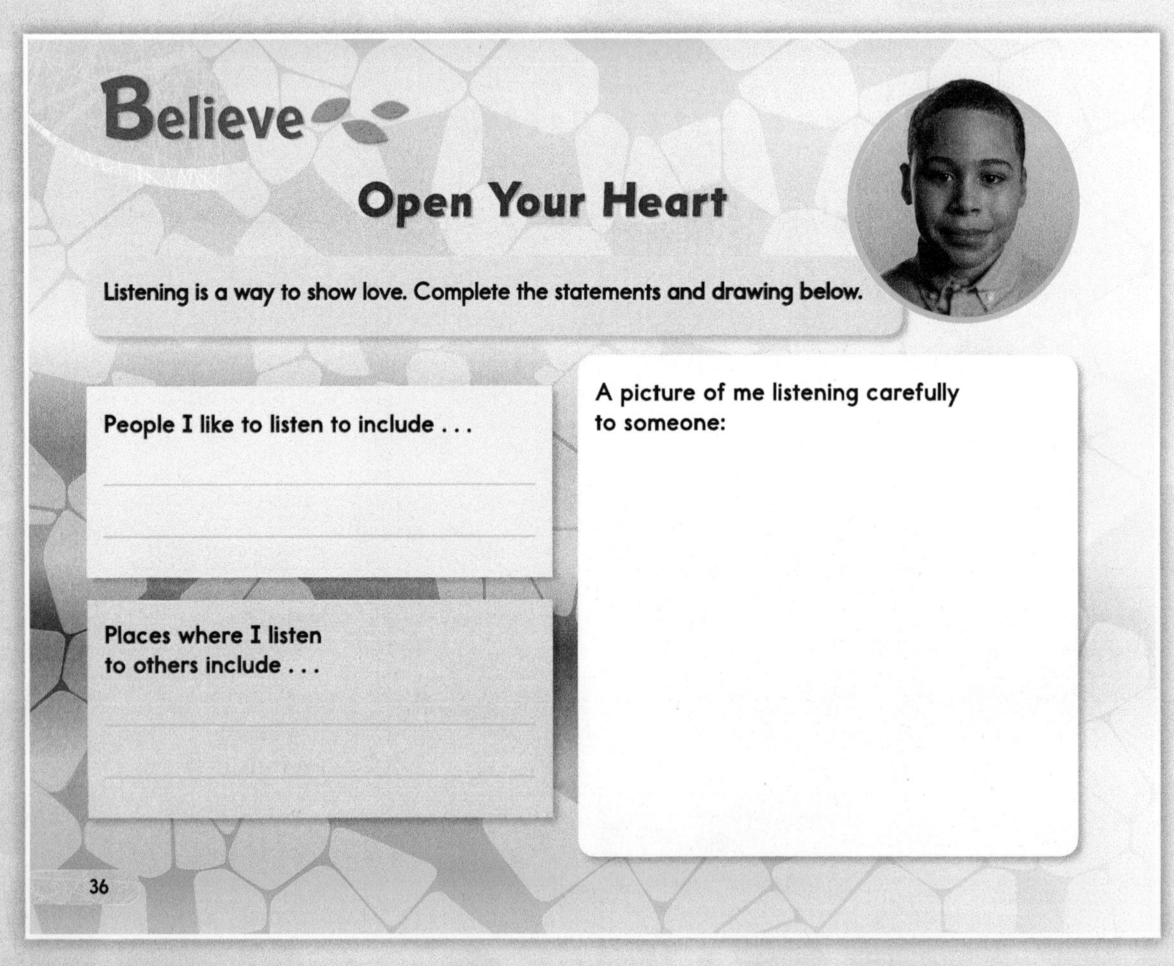
Believe
Open Your Heart
Listening is a way to show love. Complete the statements and drawing below.
People I like to listen to include . . .
Places where I listen to others include . . .
A picture of me listening carefully to someone:
36

When God Speaks

Invite the children to recall the pictures they drew of themselves as good listeners. Ask: *What helps you to pay close attention to someone who is speaking?*

Read the first paragraph on why it is important to listen carefully.

Ask *What is it like when someone listens to you and responds to what you said?*

Read the remaining text. Ask: *Why does God want us to listen carefully to Scripture?*

Direct attention to the photograph on this page. Say: *Just as sunlight and water help plants to grow, reading and listening to the Word of God help us to grow in our understanding of God's love for us.*

Share the Scripture quote. Then read it together. Ask: *What should we do after we listen to the Word of God?*

Activity

- Invite the children to imagine that God just told them something important and they understood exactly what God meant!
- Distribute drawing paper and crayons, and invite the children to draw a picture showing God's message to them. Remind them to give their picture a title.
- Conclude by having the children close their eyes. Ask: *How will God's message change the way you will live?*

Notes

When God Speaks

There are good reasons why we listen. Listening is a way to learn. It shows that we care. But good listeners do more than hear words. A careful listener also tries to understand what is said and responds in some way.

What is it like when someone listens to you and responds to what you said?

"Be doers of the word and not hearers only."

God invites us to listen to him. At Mass, God speaks to us in the readings we hear from Scripture. These readings help us to understand God better. Like a plant needs water and sunshine to grow, we need the Word of God to grow in faith, hope, and love.

When you hear the Word of God at Mass, listen with attention and an open mind and heart. Know that God is speaking to you. Respond by giving thanks to God for his love. Then go and share the truth of God's love with others.

Believe

The Word of the Lord

Share that in the time of Jesus many people were farmers. They knew a great deal about planting seeds.

Read aloud the introductory paragraph before the Scripture.

Explain that the children are about to listen to a story that Jesus told called a parable, which uses the idea of planting seeds to teach people a very important lesson about listening to the Word of God.

Guide the children through an adaptation of *Lectio Divina*, a special way to pray with Scripture. Quiet the children, and ask them to listen carefully to the Scripture reading as you read it aloud.

Reflect on the reading by inviting the children to:

- Take a moment to think about what they heard.
- Silently answer the following questions for reflection (be sure to pause after each question): *What word or words did you hear? What do you think Jesus is saying to you?*
- Quietly hold these words in their hearts. (Pause in prayer.)
- Share aloud in one or two words what they heard. Describe what they were feeling in their hearts. (Accept all responses.)

Guide the children through an adaptation of *Visio Divina*, a special way to pray with Scripture art. Quiet the children, and invite them to take their time looking at the illustration on pages 38 and 39. Read aloud the Scripture once again. Invite the children to silently answer these questions: *What do you see? What does it mean to you? What do you imagine Jesus inviting you to see? What do you think this means for you?*

Believe

The Word of the Lord

One day a large crowd gathered to hear Jesus teach. Jesus told them this story. You can read this story with your friends and family, too.

Based on MATTHEW 13:3–8, 23

Once a farmer went out to his fields and scattered seeds. Some seeds did not fall in his field. They fell on a path. Birds came and ate these seeds. Some seeds fell on rocky ground. The soil was not very deep. Plants began to grow. But then they dried up and died. Other seeds fell into the thorns and weeds. Plants started to grow. But the thorns and weeds choked these plants.

"But some seed fell on rich soil." (Matthew 13:8) These seeds grew into strong, healthy plants and produced fruit.

Jesus explained the meaning of his story. He said that people who listen carefully to the Word of God are like the seeds in the rich soil. They grow in God's love and share his love with others.

Share After the silent reflection, allow time for sharing aloud responses to these questions. Then invite the children to look again at the picture and silently answer the questions: *What are some things this picture tells you about growing? What helps us to grow in God's love?* Invite volunteers to share their responses aloud.

Check comprehension by asking: *Which seeds grow into strong, healthy plants?* (seeds that fall on rich soil) *How can we be like seeds in rich soil for God's Word?* (We can listen carefully to the Word of God and grow in God's love and share it with others.)

Share with the children the explanation in the Scripture Background. Ask: *What are some ways we can show we have listened with our hearts to the Word of God?* (pray, worship at Mass, share the Word of God with others, and care for others)

Scripture Background

After he told the Parable of the Sower, Jesus explained the meaning of the parable:

- The seeds that fell on the path are like people who learn what Jesus taught us about God's love but do not accept Jesus' message.
- The seeds that fell on rocky ground are like people who give up living as Jesus' followers because they think it is too hard to do so.
- The seeds that fell among thorns and weeds are like people who are selfish and care too much about the things they own.
- The seeds that fell on rich soil are like people who listen to the Word of God with their hearts. They worship God on the Lord's Day, share their time and their things with others, care for others, and take care of God's gift of creation.

Celebrate

Proclaiming the Word of the Lord

Ask *What do you remember about the Introductory Rites of the Mass?* Then explain that today the group will talk about the Liturgy of the Word. Write *Liturgy of the Word* on the board. Point to the word *liturgy*. Share the following: "The word 'liturgy' originally meant a 'public work' or a 'service in the name of/on behalf of the people.' In Christian tradition it means the participation of the People of God in 'the work of God'" (*CCC*, 1069).

Invite sharing about what we know about the Bible. Then read aloud the text on page 40. Make two columns on chart paper, and write the heading *Old Testament* on one side and *New Testament* on the other.

Ask *What do we learn from the Old Testament? from the New Testament?* Write responses on the chart paper.

Share about where and when we listen to the Word of God. Emphasize that the Word of God is proclaimed at every celebration of the Eucharist, the Mass.

Catholic Faith and Life

Point out the list of the parts of the Liturgy of the Word on page 40. Ask: *Why do you think the Word of God is proclaimed at every Mass?* Guide the discussion to the understanding that the Word of God is an important part of our faith as Catholics. Say, "God is with us in his Word. The Word of God teaches us how to live as his children."

CATHOLIC IDENTITY

Read the statement together. Pray aloud: *May the Word of God guide me in all that I do and say.*

Notes ______________________________

____

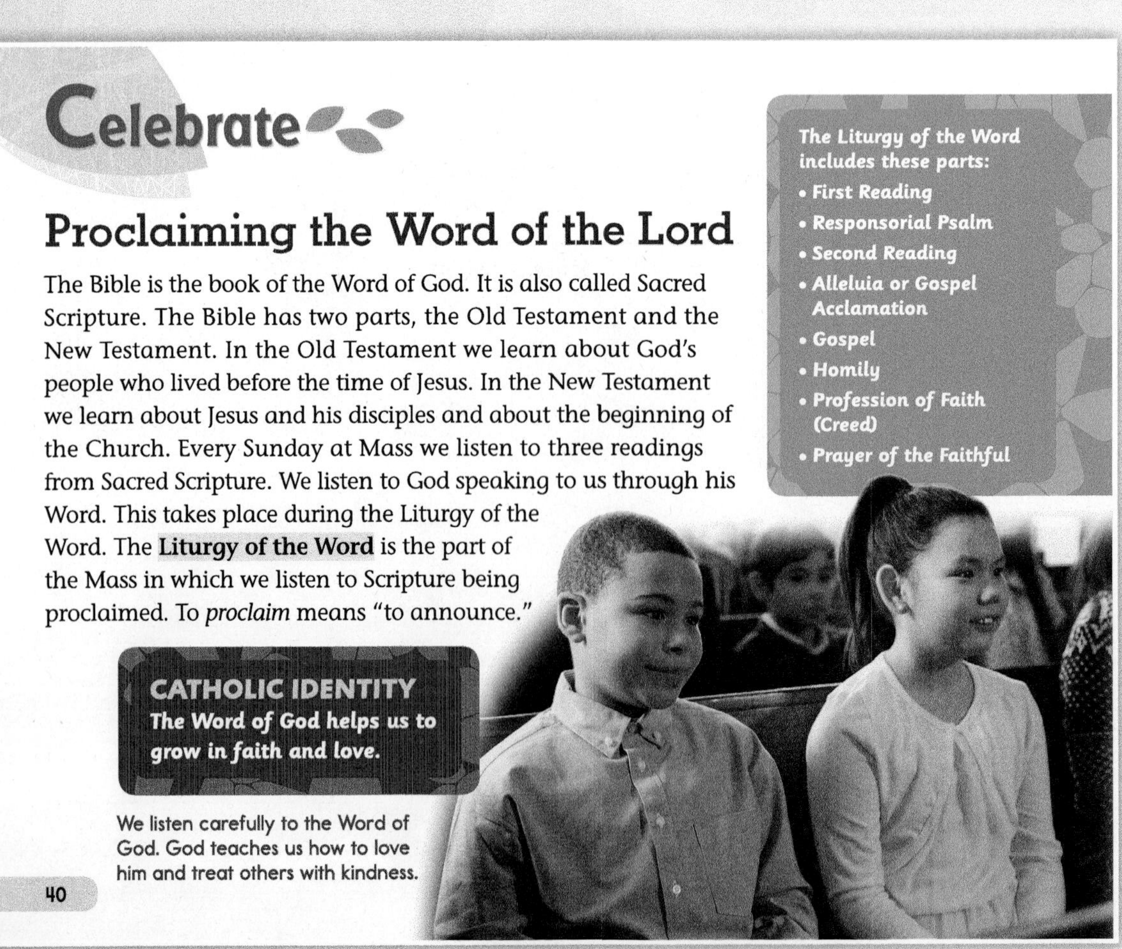

Celebrate

Proclaiming the Word of the Lord

The Bible is the book of the Word of God. It is also called Sacred Scripture. The Bible has two parts, the Old Testament and the New Testament. In the Old Testament we learn about God's people who lived before the time of Jesus. In the New Testament we learn about Jesus and his disciples and about the beginning of the Church. Every Sunday at Mass we listen to three readings from Sacred Scripture. We listen to God speaking to us through his Word. This takes place during the Liturgy of the Word. The **Liturgy of the Word** is the part of the Mass in which we listen to Scripture being proclaimed. To *proclaim* means "to announce."

The Liturgy of the Word includes these parts:
- First Reading
- Responsorial Psalm
- Second Reading
- Alleluia or Gospel Acclamation
- Gospel
- Homily
- Profession of Faith (Creed)
- Prayer of the Faithful

CATHOLIC IDENTITY
The Word of God helps us to grow in faith and love.

We listen carefully to the Word of God. God teaches us how to love him and treat others with kindness.

40

Read aloud page 41. Ask these or similar questions: *How many readings from the Bible are proclaimed at Sunday Mass?* (three) *What does the word* gospel *mean?* (The word *gospel* means "good news.") *What good news do we hear in the Gospel?* (We hear the Good News about Jesus Christ and his teachings.)

Explain that Jesus is present in his Word.

Direct attention to the photograph. Ask: *Who is proclaiming the Gospel?* Explain that only a priest or deacon proclaims the Gospel at Mass. We stand as we listen to the Gospel to honor Jesus, our Savior.

Activity

Introduce children to the gesture we make before the Gospel is proclaimed. When the priest or deacon announces the Gospel, we trace the cross with our thumb on our forehead, lips, and heart.

This gesture is a form of prayer, asking that the Word of God be in our thoughts, words, and hearts. Practice the gesture together.

Words of Faith

Liturgy of the Word (page 40)

psalm (page 41)

Gospel (page 41)

Celebrating Cultural Diversity

Traditions and customs from cultures that make up our one Church

In India, Syro-Malabar Catholics demonstrate a deep love of Scripture. Families often gather for prayer in their homes, and they read Scripture and spend time together in silent prayer. Family prayer is usually before or after the evening meal and often takes place in a prayer space or shrine set up in a special area in the home. These prayer spaces may be adorned with images of Jesus, the Blessed Virgin Mary, or saints.

On most Sundays the first reading is from the Old Testament. From this reading we learn what God did for the Jewish People before Jesus was born. We learn that God's love for his people never ends. The Responsorial Psalm is our response to the first reading. A cantor sings or a reader proclaims the psalm. We sing or say a response. A **psalm** is a song of praise from the Old Testament.

The Gospel has a place of honor in the Liturgy of the Word, so we stand when the priest or deacon proclaims the Gospel.

The second reading is from the New Testament. During this reading we listen to the teachings of the Apostles and other disciples. We learn about the beginning of the Church.

The third reading is the **Gospel**. The Gospels are four books of the New Testament that tell about Jesus' life and teachings. The word *gospel* means "good news." On most Sundays we sing *Alleluia* before the Gospel is read. When we listen to the Gospel, we learn the Good News about Jesus Christ and how to live as his disciples.

Throughout the year, as the Church proclaims the readings at Mass, we remember and celebrate the whole mystery of Christ. We celebrate the Incarnation, or the Son of God becoming man, and the Nativity, or the birth of Jesus. We celebrate Jesus' Death, Resurrection, and Ascension, his sending of the Holy Spirit on Pentecost, and his coming again at the end of time.

Celebrate

Responding to the Word of God

Share what a treasure the Word of God is. We can listen and respond to the Word of God at every Mass!

Read the first three sentences on page 42 and practice the responses. Explain that we are also responding to the Word of God when we bring God's peace and love to others.

Read aloud the explanation of the homily. Ask: *Why is the homily an important part of the Liturgy of the Word?* (In the homily the priest or deacon helps us to understand what the readings have to do with our lives today. He helps us to see ways we can share God's love with others.)

Read aloud the text on the Creed. Ask: *What do we proclaim when we pray the Creed at Mass?* (We profess the faith of the Church.)

Have the children turn to page 93 in their books to pray together the Apostles' Creed. Following the prayer, point out the beliefs we express in the Creed. Share also that the Nicene Creed, which we usually pray at Mass, can be found on page 13 of the *Believe—Celebrate—Live* resource *My Mass Book*.

Activity

- Invite the children to play a game that will help them to identify where the readings/responses at Mass come from. Distribute paper cut-out circles, two per child. Ask the children to write *OT* (Old Testament) on one circle, and *NT* (New Testament) on the other.
- List the following on chart paper: *First Reading, Responsorial Psalm, Second Reading, Gospel.* Be sure to keep the list for later use. Invite the children to show which part of the Bible each comes from by holding up either the "OT" or "NT" sign as you call out each reading or response.

Responding to the Word of God

We praise and thank God during the Liturgy of the Word. After the first and second readings, we pray, "Thanks be to God." After the Gospel, we pray, "Praise to you, Lord Jesus Christ." After we have heard all the readings, the priest or deacon talks to us about them. This talk is called the **homily**. When we listen carefully to the homily, we learn more about God. We learn ways we can share God's love with others. When the homily is finished, we pray the **Creed**. In the Creed we proclaim the faith of the Church. We believe in God the Father, God the Son, and God the Holy Spirit. We believe in the Church and in God's forgiveness of our sins.

During the Liturgy of the Word, we pray the Creed, a prayer stating what we believe as Catholics.

The parish community listens to the readings from Sacred Scripture.

Read the first paragraph, about the Prayer of the Faithful. Invite the children to name the pope, the leader of the Catholic Church, and the local bishop, who is the leader of the diocese, for whom we pray at Mass.

Share examples of other people we pray for at Mass. Then explain that in the Prayer of the Faithful we pray for the needs of all God's people. Since this is the last part of the Liturgy of the Word, you may wish to have the children turn to page 40 to review all the parts of the Liturgy of the Word. Then prepare to take a closer look at the people and things connected with the Liturgy of the Word in the remaining text on page 43.

Direct the children to review the list you saved on chart paper. Recall with the children that these are the readings proclaimed during the Liturgy of the Word. Draw a simple outline of an ambo below the list. Explain that every Scripture reading at Mass is proclaimed from this sacred reading stand.

Read the text that begins "In the Liturgy of the Word." Write "First Reading," "Second Reading," and "Gospel" on the board or chart paper. Write the word *lector* or *reader* next to "First Reading" and "Second Reading" on the list. Explain that the lector or reader reads from a book called the Lectionary. Write *priest* or *deacon* next to "Gospel." Explain that the priest or deacon reads from the *Book of Gospels*. You may want to call attention to the photo on page 28. Point out that the deacon is carrying the *Book of the Gospels*. On page 41, the deacon is reading from it.

Words of Faith

Homily (page 42)
Creed (page 42)
Prayer of the Faithful (page 43)
lector (page 43)
Lectionary (page 43)
ambo (page 43)
Book of the Gospels (page 43)

After the Creed we pray the **Prayer of the Faithful**. In the Prayer of the Faithful, we pray for the needs of the Church. We pray for the pope, other Church leaders, and all God's people. We pray for world leaders. We pray for people throughout the world, especially for those who are sick or in need. We pray for the people in our parish who have died. We pray for people in our lives who need God's love and help. After each prayer, we ask God to hear our prayer.

In the Liturgy of the Word:

- A reader, or **lector**, reads the first two readings. They are read from a book called the **Lectionary**. The lector stands at the **ambo** to read. An ambo is a sacred reading stand, the Table of the Word of God. We sit and listen to the readings.
- A priest or deacon stands at the ambo to read from the Gospel of Matthew, Mark, Luke, or John. The Gospel is most often read from a special book called the **Book of the Gospels**. We stand as the Gospel is read because the Gospel has a place of honor in the Liturgy of the Word.

During the Liturgy of the Word, God speaks to us through Sacred Scripture. Sacred Scripture is proclaimed from the *ambo*, or "Table of the Word of God."

Live

Become What You Believe

Explain that the different Scripture readings that we hear at Mass help us to understand more about God—Father, Son, and Holy Spirit. Through listening to the Word of God, we experience God's great love for us. Hold up a Bible or Lectionary, the Word of God. Have the children read together the sentence at the top of page 44.

Direct attention to the statement in bold at the bottom of the page. Ask the group to read it aloud together. Explain that the strength we receive from the Word of God helps us to be good disciples of Jesus Christ. Invite the children to reflect and share what this means for their lives.

Activity

Read aloud the bold heads. Use the following guide to help the children write their responses.

What I learn by listening to the Word of God: Invite the children to share what they learn about God, about themselves, and about others from listening to the Word of God.

Ways I respond to the Word of God: Remind the children that they respond to the Word of God at Mass. They also respond to the Word of God by the way they live. Have the children suggest ways they can live as good disciples.

Notes ______________________

____

____

Live

Become What You Believe

I listen to the Word of God at Mass.

What I learn by listening to the Word of God:

____

Ways I respond to the Word of God:

____

The Word of God gives me strength.

Discipleship in Action

Read aloud the story of Saint Benedict on page 45. Talk about what Saint Benedict did so he could better hear God speak to him.

Share that we too can find ways to read Scripture and reflect on the Word of God. Wherever we are, the Holy Spirit helps us to understand Sacred Scripture.

Explain the meaning of the word *reflect* as a way to think about and imagine something important. People often sit in a quiet place to reflect. Have the children picture a quiet place in their homes or outdoors where they could reflect on the Word of God. Recall with the children that the Word of God helps us to follow Jesus' example of love.

Activity

- Read aloud the sentence starters. Have the children reflect on where and when they listen to the Word of God. Direct the children to write what they do to listen to the Word of God. Then have them write one way they can share the Word of God with others.
- Say aloud the beginning of the Scripture verse from James 1:22 on page 37: "Be doers of the word and not. . . ." Pause to let the children say the rest of the verse. You may point to your ears to prompt them to say "hearers only."

Notes ______________________

____

____

____

Discipleship in Action

Saint Benedict (A.D. 480–547)

Saint Benedict was from a wealthy family in the busy city of Rome. As a young adult, he became unhappy with this life and wanted to become holier. So, he left Rome for a quiet place in the mountains. Once there, he lived alone. He devoted himself to strengthening his relationship with God. He read Scripture, prayed, and reflected in silence. After a few years, Benedict was chosen to lead a group of monks. He led the monastic community to seek the glory of God through a life of listening and reflecting on the Word of God.

I listen to the Word of God in my life by . . .

____

____

I can share the Word of God with others by . . .

____

____

Lord, Hear My Prayer/*Oyenos, Señor*

Read and familiarize yourself with the prayer and the music selection. To prepare the environment, arrange the following items on a small table:

- white tablecloth
- crucifix
- Bible on a table stand

You will also need:

- CD player
- Music CD, queued to play the track "Lord, Hear My Prayer"

Invite the children to gather around the table with their books. Share that the Spanish words *Oyenos, Señor* in the song mean "Hear us, Lord." Teach the children the song. Direct attention to the part of the prayer where the children will be asked to pray a prayer of their own. Share an example of an intention: "For my friend who is sick." The children may follow your lead when it is time to pray for their own intentions. (Note: The refrain will resume after a few minutes.) Pray the prayer together, ending with the Lord's Prayer (page 93 of child's book).

Conclude the prayer ritual with the following "mystagogy," or reflection on the experience. Invite the children to give one- or two- word responses to the following:

- *What feeling did you have when you offered your own prayer?*
- *Is it hard to pray in front of others?*
- *What was it like to sing in English and in Spanish?*
- *Why do we sing in different languages?*

Notes ______________________________

____

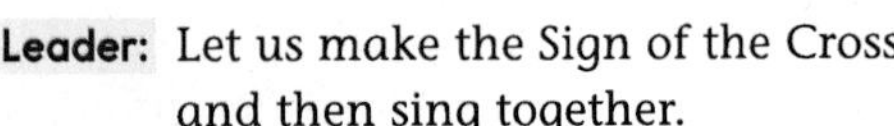

Lord, Hear My Prayer/ *Oyenos, Señor*

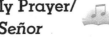

Leader: Let us make the Sign of the Cross and then sing together.

All: (*Refrain*) Lord, hear our prayer. *Oyenos, Señor*. Lord, hear our prayer. *Oyenos, Señor*.

Leader: For the holy Church, that the Lord watch over her and care for her, let us pray to the Lord.

All: (*Sing refrain.*)

Leader: For the peoples of all the world, that the Lord may unite and bless them, let us pray to the Lord.

All: (*Sing refrain.*)

Leader: For all who need care and healing, that the Lord will help them, let us pray to the Lord.

All: (*Sing refrain.*)

Leader: For our families, our friends, our neighbors, and ourselves, that the Lord will hear all of our prayers, let us pray to the Lord.

All: (*Sing refrain.*)

Leader: At this time, I invite you to offer a prayer of your own.

All: (*Sing refrain.*)

Leader: Let us join hands and pray as Jesus taught us.

All: Our Father . . .

46

Living Faith at Home

Encourage family participation by having the children take home the double-sided "Living Faith at Home" page.

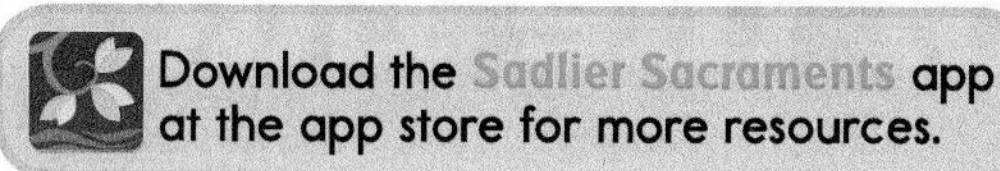

Living Faith at Home

"But some seed fell on rich soil."

MATTHEW 13:8

Take a few minutes to reflect on the Scripture art. Ask God to open your eyes and your heart. What feelings are you experiencing? What do you understand from the image about growing? In what ways do you grow? What else do you see? Pray a silent prayer of gratitude.

 47

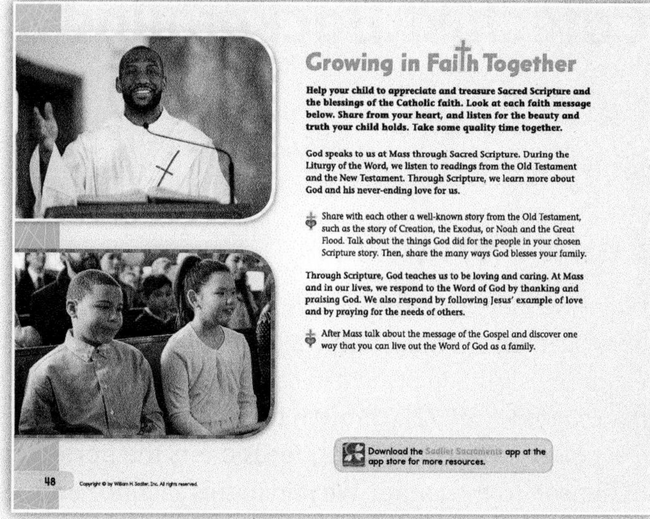

Growing in Faith Together

Help your child to appreciate and treasure Sacred Scripture and the blessings of the Catholic faith. Look at each faith message below. Share from your heart, and listen for the beauty and truth your child holds. Take some quality time together.

God speaks to us at Mass through Sacred Scripture. During the Liturgy of the Word, we listen to readings from the Old Testament and the New Testament. Through Scripture, we learn more about God and his never-ending love for us.

- Share with each other a well-known story from the Old Testament, such as the story of Creation, the Exodus, or Noah and the Great Flood. Talk about the things God did for the people in your chosen Scripture story. Then, share the many ways God blesses your family.

Through Scripture, God teaches us to be loving and caring. At Mass and in our lives, we respond to the Word of God by thanking and praising God. We also respond by following Jesus' example of love and by praying for the needs of others.

- After Mass talk about the message of the Gospel and discover one way that you can live out the Word of God as a family.

Download the Sadlier Sacraments app at the app store for more resources.

48

Celebrating Inclusion

Strategies and tips for including children with disabilities

Use the following tips to teach this chapter through a multisensory approach, which may benefit not only children with learning differences but others as well. The more we teach in a multisensory approach that includes auditory, visual, and tactile-kinesthetic (hands-on) opportunities for learning, the more learners we will reach when we teach.

Believe On page 36, Allow children who have difficulty writing or who lack fine motor skills to respond verbally.

Children who prefer hands-on activities will enjoy having a plant to water as depicted on page 37.

For page 38, auditory learners will enjoy a recording of the Scripture to listen to multiple times. On pages 38 and 39, visual learners will benefit from closely looking at and discussing the art depicting the Parable of the Sower. Have tactile-kinesthetic learners act out what happens to each seed: Seeds on the path get eaten by birds; seeds on rocks just lie there because they can't spread roots; seeds in weeds get choked (have children scrunch shoulders); seeds on good soil grow (have children spread arms and slowly stand up to grow).

Celebrate On page 40, provide children who prefer hands-on activities with a Bible to hold and open. Have partners locate where the Old Testament ends and the New Testament begins.

On page 43, support hands-on learners by having the children work in groups to create their own Prayer of the Faithful. If possible, take the children to the church or chapel to read their prayers from the ambo.

Live On pages 44 and 45, allow children who have difficulty writing to respond verbally.

On page 46, visual learners will benefit from having pictures that depict what is being prayed. Provide children who have reading difficulties with a blank sheet of paper to cover the words that appear below the sentence being read to help them focus. During the Lord's Prayer, allow children who prefer not to hold hands to opt out, or to hold out their hands, palms up, instead.

Notes ______________________________

____

Celebrating the Liturgy of the Eucharist

Catechist Background

Faith Focus

Jesus is with me!

Faith Formation

When we celebrate the Liturgy of the Eucharist, our attention is focused on the altar. At the altar, "the Sacrifice of the Cross is continuously made present in the Church" (*General Instruction of the Roman Missal*, 72). Through the ministry of the priest and by the power of the Holy Spirit, Jesus offers the perfect sacrifice of himself to the Father. We join in this sacrifice and also offer ourselves—our challenges and successes in living as followers of Jesus Christ—to the Father.

To begin the Liturgy of the Eucharist, we bring to the altar the gifts of bread and wine; Jesus used these to institute the Sacrament of the Eucharist at the Last Supper. Following the Preparation of the Gifts, the priest prays the Church's greatest prayer of praise and thanksgiving. This prayer is called the Eucharistic Prayer. We kneel in reverent and attentive silence as the priest offers this prayer in the name of the entire community. Together we glorify God and thank him for his great love and mercy.

The priest prays the prayer of Consecration, transforming the gifts of bread and wine into the Body and Blood of Christ by the power of the Holy Spirit. What looks and tastes like bread and wine has become the Body and Blood of Christ. We understand Jesus Christ to be really present in the Eucharist under the appearance of bread and wine. This is known as the Real Presence.

As you present the chapter, share the mystery of the Eucharist with joy. Recall the words of Consecration in which the priest follows the same words and actions that Jesus did when he first gave us the greatest gift of love—his own Body and Blood.

For Personal Reflection

Do I pay close attention to the actions and words of the priest during the Eucharistic Prayer? Am I fully aware of Jesus' Real Presence in the Eucharist, and how do I welcome him into my heart?

Catechist Prayer

O Lord, help me to guide the children to your altar. Open their eyes to the beautiful gift of the Sacrament of the Body and Blood of Jesus Christ.

Resources

Roman Missal

Catechism of the Catholic Church, 1329, 1333, 1345–1355,1353, 1360, 1365, 1380, 1407, 1408, 1409, 1411, 1412, 1413

We Believe, Catholic Identity Edition, Grade 2, Chapters 15 and 18

Believe—Celebrate—Live: Eucharist DVD, Chapter 4 video; Music CD, "Our God Is Here"

Celebrating Inclusion

Strategies and tips for including children with disabilities are found on page 61–62.

Words of Faith 

- Last Supper
- altar
- Liturgy of the Eucharist
- sacrifice
- Eucharistic Prayer
- Consecration
- paten
- chalice
- Real Presence

CHAPTER 4

Introduce the Chapter

Review the lesson introduction on page 49.

Play the video segment introducing the chapter. Alternatively, share the story below.

Read-Aloud Story (Optional)

Kate

I like to listen and pay attention. When I go to Mass, I try to pay attention and discover something new. So much seems to be happening at the altar! I especially like the part when Father William consecrates the bread and wine.

First he holds up a large Host and says, "THIS IS MY BODY." I know now that Father William is speaking in Jesus' name. The Host still looks like ordinary bread, but it is not! Jesus is now with us in an extraordinary way. The bread has become the Body of Christ.

Then Father William raises the chalice of wine and says, "THIS IS THE CHALICE OF MY BLOOD." The wine has become the Blood of Christ. And I remember that Jesus died on the Cross for our sins. Like the rest of my parish family, I don't say anything out loud during this part of the Mass, except for when we sing or say the responses and acclamations. But when I follow Father William's words and actions, I am participating in Jesus' offering of himself at the altar.

Through the ages, a lot of people have joined in this great prayer that Jesus first prayed with his disciples at the Last Supper. Now I can join in, too!

- **What did I learn by listening and paying attention at Mass?**

Celebrating the Liturgy of the Eucharist

Chapter Planner

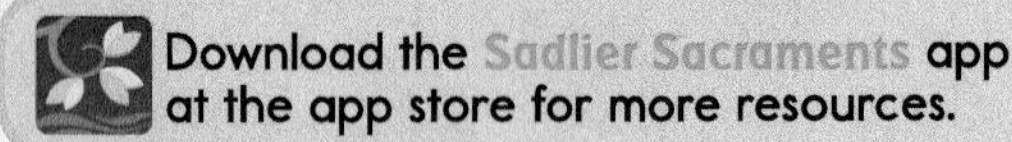
Download the Sadlier Sacraments app at the app store for more resources.

Time	Materials	Steps
Believe pages 49–53		
15–20 minutes	• battery-operated candle • Chapter 4 video • Bible open to the Scripture passage on page 52, for direct reading of the Scripture	• Pray the words from the *Roman Missal.* • View and discuss the Chapter 4 video (or share the Read-Aloud Story, page 49B). • Complete the activity. • Discuss the photographs. • Read and discuss the text. • Read aloud the Scripture story of the Last Supper, and engage in the *Lectio* and *Visio Divina* exercise.
Celebrate pages 54–57		
20–30 minutes	• props to represent the cruets and the paten, the gifts brought to the altar during the Mass • picture of the Last Supper (optional) • clay or modeling dough, for making replicas of a chalice and a paten	• Present the text. • Discuss the photographs and captions. • Complete the activities. • Present the "Catholic Identity" and "Catholic Faith and Life" features. • Discuss the Words of Faith. • Present the "Celebrating Cultural Diversity" feature.
Live pages 58–60		
10–15 minutes	• prayer space materials listed on page 60 • *Believe—Celebrate—Live* Music CD • world map (optional)	• Prepare the prayer space. • Discuss ways Jesus is with you. • Complete the activity. • Read and respond to the "Discipleship in Action" story and activity. • Pray and sing "Our God Is Here." • Close with reflection questions. • Remind the children to bring home the "Living Faith at Home" page.

Key: 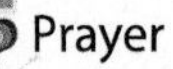 Prayer  Video  Scripture 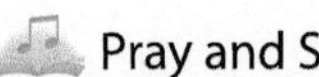 Pray and Sing

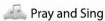

Introduce the Chapter

Celebrating the Liturgy of the Eucharist

Welcome the children and tell them that they will hear about Jesus' most precious gift to us.

Gather for prayer. Light a battery-operated candle. Then pray together the Sign of the Cross. Call attention to the verse on page 49, from the *Roman Missal*. Proclaim the words together.

Share that we pray this prayer at Mass after the priest prays over the gifts of bread and wine that will become the Body and Blood of Christ.

Direct attention to the photograph.

Ask *What is this family sharing together?*

Share with the children that our parish family gathers for a very special meal at Mass.

Introduce the video segment for this chapter by saying, "Let's explore some of the themes of this chapter with our young friends from the chapter video." Play the video.

Alternatively, you may choose to share the Read-Aloud Story found on page 49B of this guide.

Notes ______________________

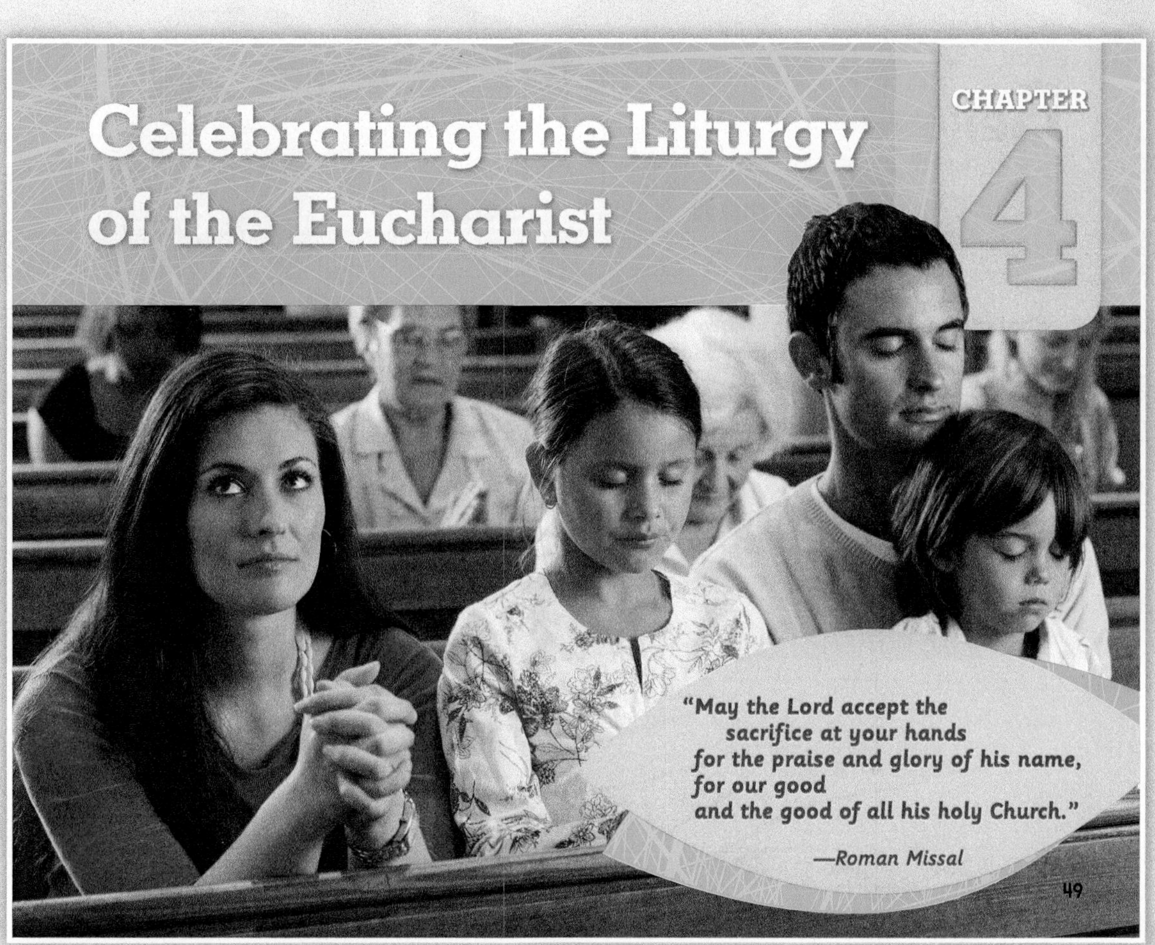

Celebrating the Liturgy of the Eucharist
CHAPTER 4
"May the Lord accept the
sacrifice at your hands
for the praise and glory of his name,
for our good
and the good of all his holy Church."
—Roman Missal
49

Believe

Open Your Heart

Ask the children the following or similar questions about what they saw in the video or heard in the Read-Aloud Story:

What happens to the gifts of bread and wine on the altar?

Why are there special words and actions for this part of the Mass?

What did you see or hear that was different or new to you?

Activity

- Share that there are many types of gifts that we can give to others. Some gifts can be put in bags or boxes. Some gifts cannot be wrapped. Challenge the children to suggest what kinds of gifts cannot be wrapped.
- Read aloud the activity directions and let the children write ways they give to others. Explain that when we look at or use a gift that someone gave us, we often think of the person who gave it to us. Call on volunteers to share a way of giving to others.

Notes

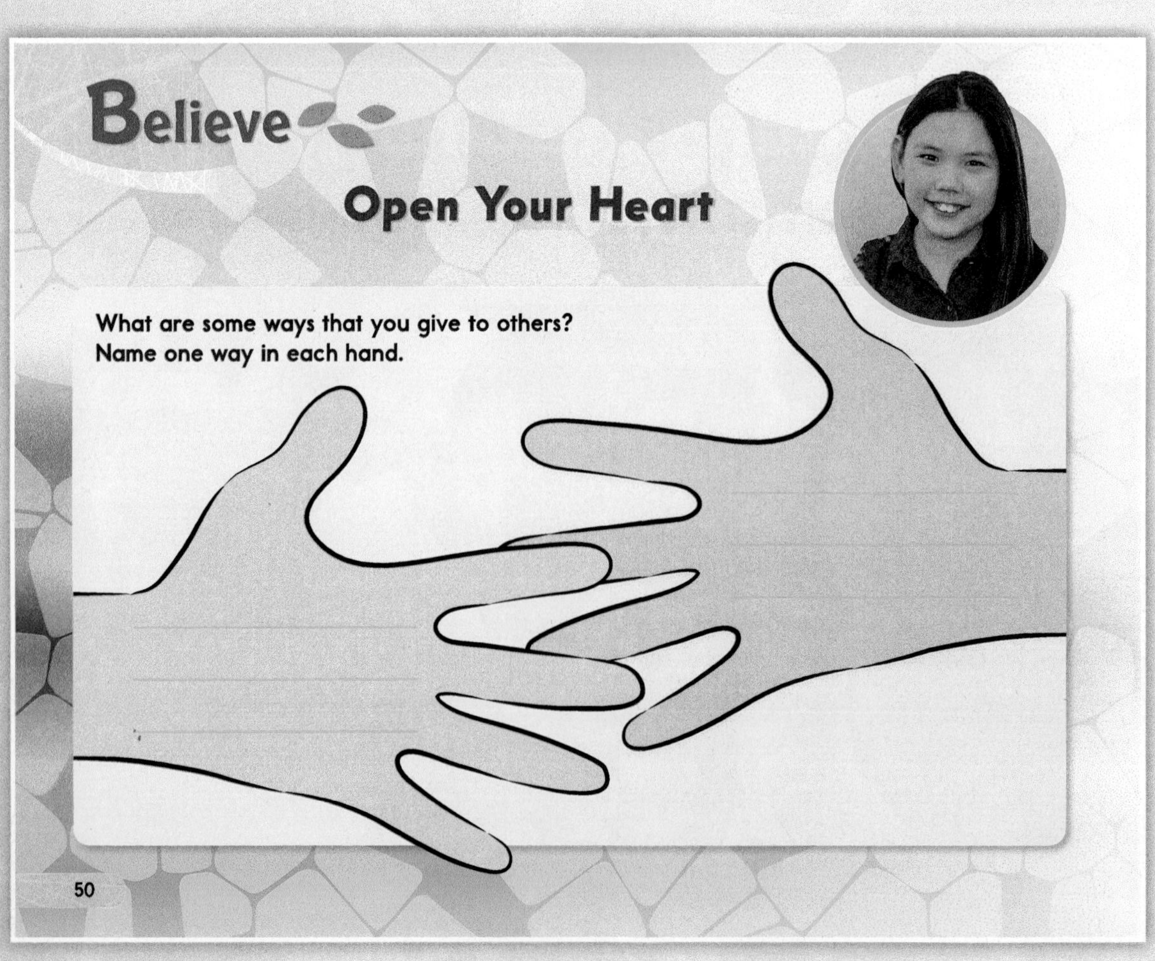

A Gift of Love

Direct attention to the photographs on page 51. Give the children time to look at and think about the photos.

Invite the children to think about their own family celebrations.

Ask the questions in the first paragraph as a way to discuss their experiences of giving and receiving gifts.

Share a gift that you received from someone. Explain that when you look at or use the gift, you think of the person who gave it to you.

Invite the children to silently think of a special gift they received and to remember who gave it to them.

Read aloud the second paragraph.

Ask *What is the gift that Jesus gives and that we receive at the celebration of the Eucharist?*

Read the Scripture quote from Luke's Gospel together. Share that we hear these words in the Liturgy of the Eucharist. Each time we receive Jesus' gift of himself, we remember God's boundless love for us.

Notes ______________________

A Gift of Love

At what special times does your family give and receive gifts? What is it like for you to give a gift? What is it like to receive a gift?

Giving and receiving gifts is a way to show love. As Catholics, every time we participate in the celebration of the Eucharist we receive the greatest gift of love: the gift of Jesus himself. With joy in our hearts, we give thanks to God for the gift of his Son, Jesus.

"Do this in memory of me."

LUKE 22:19

Believe

The Word of the Lord

Share the meaning of the Jewish feast of Passover and the Last Supper from the "Scripture Background" feature on page 53.

Read aloud the introductory paragraph before the Scripture. This will reinforce the essential background information.

Explain that the children are going to hear a reading from the Bible, the living Word of God. This Scripture passage tells us what happened at Jesus' last Passover feast with his Apostles according to the Gospel of Mark.

Guide the children through an adaptation of *Lectio Divina*, a special way to pray with Scripture. Quiet the children, and ask them to listen carefully to the Scripture reading as you read it aloud.

Reflect on the reading by inviting the children to:

- Take a moment to think about what they heard.
- Silently answer the following questions for reflection (be sure to pause after each question): *What word or words did you hear? What do you think Jesus is saying to you?*
- Quietly hold these words in their hearts. (Pause in prayer.)
- Share aloud in one or two words what they heard. Describe what they were feeling in their hearts. (Accept all responses.)

Guide the children through an adaptation of *Visio Divina*, a special way to pray with Scripture art. Quiet the children, and invite them to take their time looking at the illustration on pages 52 and 53. Read aloud the Scripture once again. Invite the children to silently answer these questions: *What do you see? What does it mean to you? What do you imagine Jesus inviting you to see? What do you think this means for you?*

Believe

The Word of the Lord

Passover is an important feast that the Jewish People celebrate every year. During this holy time the Jewish People gather to share a meal and remember that God led their ancestors from slavery to the Promised Land.

 Based on MARK 14:22–24

On the night before Jesus died, he and his disciples, who were Jewish, were getting ready to celebrate the Passover. Here is what Jesus said and did at the meal.

"While they were eating, he took bread, said the blessing, broke it, and gave it to them, and said, 'Take it; this is my body.' Then he took a cup, gave thanks, and gave it to them, and they all drank from it. He said to them, 'This is my blood.'" (Mark 14:22–24)

This was the last meal Jesus shared with his disciples before he died. We call this meal the **Last Supper**. At the Last Supper Jesus gave us the gift of the Eucharist. The Eucharist is the Sacrament of the Body and Blood of Jesus Christ.

52

Share After the silent reflection, allow time for sharing aloud responses to these questions. Then invite the children to look again at the picture and silently answer these questions: *What are some things this picture tells you about the Last Supper? What does it tell you about what the disciples saw and heard at this meal?* Invite volunteers to share their responses aloud.

Check comprehension by having the children enact the Last Supper as a skit. Choose children to be the narrator, Jesus, and the disciples. Guide the children in retelling the story accurately and with great reverence.

Ask *Why is the meal Jesus shared with his disciples one of the most important events in our faith?* (It was at this meal that Jesus gave the Church the Sacrament of the Eucharist.)

Why is listening to the Scripture reading about the Last Supper important to your preparation for the Sacrament of the Eucharist? (The reading reminds us that the bread and wine Jesus shared with his disciples at the Last Supper became his actual Body and Blood.)

Scripture Background

Jesus joined other Jewish People in the holy city of Jerusalem for important Jewish feasts, including the feast of Passover. As a Passover meal, the Last Supper included unleavened bread and grape wine. The loaf of bread would be broken into pieces at the table to be shared. The wine was made from grapes and was the principal drink of the Jewish People. When Jesus and his disciples gathered for this meal, they prayed and gave thanks to God. Then Jesus did something unexpected. He celebrated the first Eucharist, in which he gave us the gift of himself.

Words of Faith

Last Supper (page 52)

Celebrate

The Liturgy of the Eucharist

Share what has been learned about the Introductory Rites and the Liturgy of the Word. Review briefly what we do in each part. Then explain that today the children will be learning about the next part of the Mass, the Liturgy of the Eucharist.

Read aloud the first two paragraphs on page 54. Emphasize that the Mass is the celebration of the Sacrament of the Eucharist.

Ask *How do families prepare for special meals?* (They prepare the food. They decorate and set the table.) Then explain that at the beginning of the Liturgy of the Eucharist, the gifts of bread and wine are presented, and the altar, the Table of the Lord, is prepared.

Read aloud the third paragraph on page 54. Explain that in this chapter the children will be learning about all of the parts of the Liturgy of the Eucharist, including the Preparation of the Gifts.

Direct attention to the photograph of children presenting the gifts of bread and wine to the priest. Emphasize that it is a privilege to bring the gifts to the altar. Say: *The people bringing up the gifts act for the entire assembly.*

CATHOLIC IDENTITY

Read aloud the statement. Pray together: *Thank you, Lord, for offering yourself in the sacrifice of the Mass. Thank you for your love and forgiveness.*

Notes ______________________

____

____

Celebrate

The Liturgy of the Eucharist

Jesus told his disciples to remember what he did at the Last Supper. He told them to celebrate this special meal again and again. He said, "Do this in memory of me" (Luke 22:19). Each time we celebrate the Eucharist, we do as Jesus said.

The celebration of the Eucharist is also called the Mass. The word *eucharist* means "to give thanks." Throughout the Mass, we give thanks and praise to God. Like the disciples at the Last Supper, we gather around a table. This special table is called the **altar**. The altar is the focal point of the Liturgy of the Eucharist.

CATHOLIC IDENTITY
The Mass makes present the one sacrifice of Jesus on the Cross, who offered himself for our sins.

The **Liturgy of the Eucharist** is the part of the Mass in which the bread and wine become the Body and Blood of Jesus Christ. The Liturgy of the Eucharist begins as the priest prepares the altar. Very often members of the assembly bring forward the gifts of bread and wine. We remember the many gifts God has given to us. We offer these gifts and ourselves to God.

We ask the Lord to accept the gifts of bread and wine that we bring to the altar.

Read aloud the list of the parts of the Liturgy of the Eucharist on page 55: the Preparation of the Gifts, the Prayer over the Offerings, the Eucharistic Prayer, and the Communion Rite.

Read aloud the next paragraph on page 55. Point out that the bread at Mass is flat and has a round shape. These flat, round pieces of bread are called the Communion hosts. Religious brothers or sisters, using a special recipe, usually bake them. If possible, show some unconsecrated hosts. Explain that the wine at Mass, called altar wine, is also specially prepared.

Note: The bread or hosts are unleavened. You may want to relate the historical significance of the unleavened bread by referring to the Passover ritual (see Exodus 12:1–10). Explain that the Israelites did not have time to wait for the dough to rise before they fled Egypt.

Read aloud the remaining text. Emphasize that the Mass is a sacrifice and that Jesus' offering of himself on the Cross is the greatest sacrifice of all. The Eucharist recalls and makes present Christ's Passover--that is, the work of salvation he achieved by his life, Death, and Resurrection.

Activity

- Assume the role of the priest and stand in the front of the room.
- Invite the children to take turns processing and presenting the gifts of bread and wine with reverence. You can use props for the paten and cruets.
- Recall with the children that the priest prays a prayer of blessing over the gifts of bread and wine. Invite the children to pray together our response, "Blessed be God for ever."

Words of Faith

altar (page 54)

Liturgy of the Eucharist (page 54)

sacrifice (page 55)

The Liturgy of the Eucharist has these parts:

- Preparation of the Gifts
- Prayer over the Offerings
- Eucharistic Prayer
- Communion Rite

The priest or deacon accepts the gifts of bread and wine and places them on the altar. As he prepares the bread and wine, the priest prays special prayers. We respond: *Blessed be God for ever.* Then we pray with the priest that the Lord will accept these gifts.

Throughout the Liturgy of the Eucharist, we remember that the Mass is a sacrifice. A **sacrifice** is an offering of a gift to God. When Jesus was on earth he offered his life for us on the Cross to save us from sin. He rose from the dead on Easter Sunday so that we could live peacefully with God forever. Jesus' work of salvation through his life, Death, and Resurrection is called his Passover. It is remembered and made present in every Mass. And it is Jesus Christ himself who acts through the priest and offers the Eucharistic sacrifice.

Celebrate

The Eucharistic Prayer

Read aloud the first paragraph on page 56.

Explain that when the Eucharistic Prayer begins, the priest invites us to lift up our hearts to the Lord and give thanks and praise. We stand and pray aloud or sing the *Sanctus* (*Holy, Holy, Holy*), which says, "Blessed is he who comes in the name of the Lord. / Hosanna in the highest." After we pray these words, we kneel.

Ask *What do you remember about these words?* (The words were used to welcome Jesus to Jerusalem on the Sunday before he died. See Mark 11:9–10.)

Direct attention to the photographs of the priest as you read aloud the remaining text on page 56. Stress the need to pay close attention to the words and actions of the priest in the Eucharistic Prayer. Review the words of Consecration. Explain that the priest says the words Jesus spoke at the Last Supper.

Check comprehension by asking these questions:

What is the Eucharistic Prayer? (The Eucharistic Prayer is the center of the Mass and the Church's greatest prayer of praise and thanksgiving.)

What is the Consecration? (the part of the Eucharistic Prayer when, by the power of the Holy Spirit and through the words and actions of the priest, the bread and wine become the Body and Blood of Christ)

Activity

- Display a picture of the Last Supper.
- Have the children compare it to the photographs of the priest consecrating the bread and wine. Ask: *What is the same?* Emphasize that, like Jesus, the priest offers the gifts of bread and wine, and also repeats the same words that Jesus said at the Last Supper.
- Invite the children to read together the captions under each photograph on page 56.

Celebrate

The Eucharistic Prayer

After the gifts are prepared, we pray the Eucharistic Prayer. The **Eucharistic Prayer** is the center of the Mass and the Church's greatest prayer of praise and thanksgiving.

The priest prays the Eucharistic Prayer in the name of the whole Church. He prays to God the Father through Jesus Christ in the Holy Spirit. Through the power of the Holy Spirit the priest says and does what Jesus said and did at the Last Supper. Taking the bread the priest says:

> "Take this, all of you, and eat of it,
> for this is my Body,
> which will be given up for you."

Then taking the cup of wine he says:

> "Take this, all of you, and drink from it,
> for this is the chalice of my Blood. . . ."

This part of the Eucharistic Prayer is called the **Consecration**.

The priest prays, "For this is my Body."

The priest prays, "For this is the chalice of my Blood."

Read aloud the first paragraph, which describes the paten and the chalice. If possible, invite a parish priest to talk to the children about their celebration of First Holy Communion. Ask him to show a paten and chalice he uses at Mass.

Activity

- Provide clay or modeling dough. Have the children mold replicas of a chalice and a paten.
- Encourage the children to place their replicas in a family prayer space at home.

Read aloud the second paragraph on page 57. Explain that the changing of the bread and wine into the Body and Blood of Christ during the Consecration of the Mass is called *transubstantiation*. Emphasize that Jesus is really present in the Eucharist, just as he was present when he first gave himself to his disciples at the Last Supper. We call Jesus Christ being present in the Eucharist the Real Presence.

Read aloud the rest of the text on page 57. Then ask: *What are we saying when we pray "Amen" at the end of the Eucharistic Prayer?* ("Amen" is our response to this great prayer. "Amen" means "Yes, I believe!")

Catholic Faith and Life

Share the feature indicating that only a priest can consecrate the bread and wine. A priest receives the power to do this in the person of Jesus Christ through the Sacrament of Holy Orders.

Words of Faith

Eucharistic Prayer (page 56)
Consecration (page 56)
paten (page 57)
chalice (page 57)
Real Presence (page 57)

During the Liturgy of the Eucharist the priest uses a special plate and cup. The plate is called a **paten**. The priest places the wheat bread that becomes the Body of Christ on the paten. The cup is called a **chalice**. The priest pours the grape wine that becomes the Blood of Christ in the chalice.

Only a priest ordained through the Sacrament of Holy Orders can preside at the Eucharist and consecrate the bread and wine.

By the power of the Holy Spirit and through the words and actions of the priest, the bread and wine become the Body and Blood of Christ. In a way that we cannot fully understand, Jesus Christ is really present in the Eucharist. We call this the **Real Presence**. The changing of the bread and wine into the Body and Blood of Christ is called *transubstantiation*.

The priest invites us to proclaim our faith. We may pray:

> "When we eat this Bread and drink this Cup,
> we proclaim your Death, O Lord,
> until you come again."

We pray that the Holy Spirit will unite all who believe in Jesus. We end the Eucharistic Prayer by praying "Amen." When we do this, we are saying, "Yes, I believe." We are saying "yes" to the prayer the priest has prayed in our name.

Jesus Christ is really present in the Eucharist.

Live

Become What You Believe

Read aloud the first sentence on page 58. As a group talk about what God has done for all people. Call special attention to Jesus' gift of himself and the sacrifice he made on the Cross. Look back at the photo on page 55 and read aloud the caption that tells what happens at every Mass.

Direct attention to the statement in bold at the bottom of the page. Ask the children to read the statement aloud together and to think about what it means in their lives.

Activity

- Invite the children to think about all the gifts God has given them, such as the gift of family and the gift of our Church.
- Have them list these gifts in the thank-you note to God. Be sure they sign their name at the end of the note.
- Encourage the children to read their note to God when they say their prayers at home.

Notes ______________________________

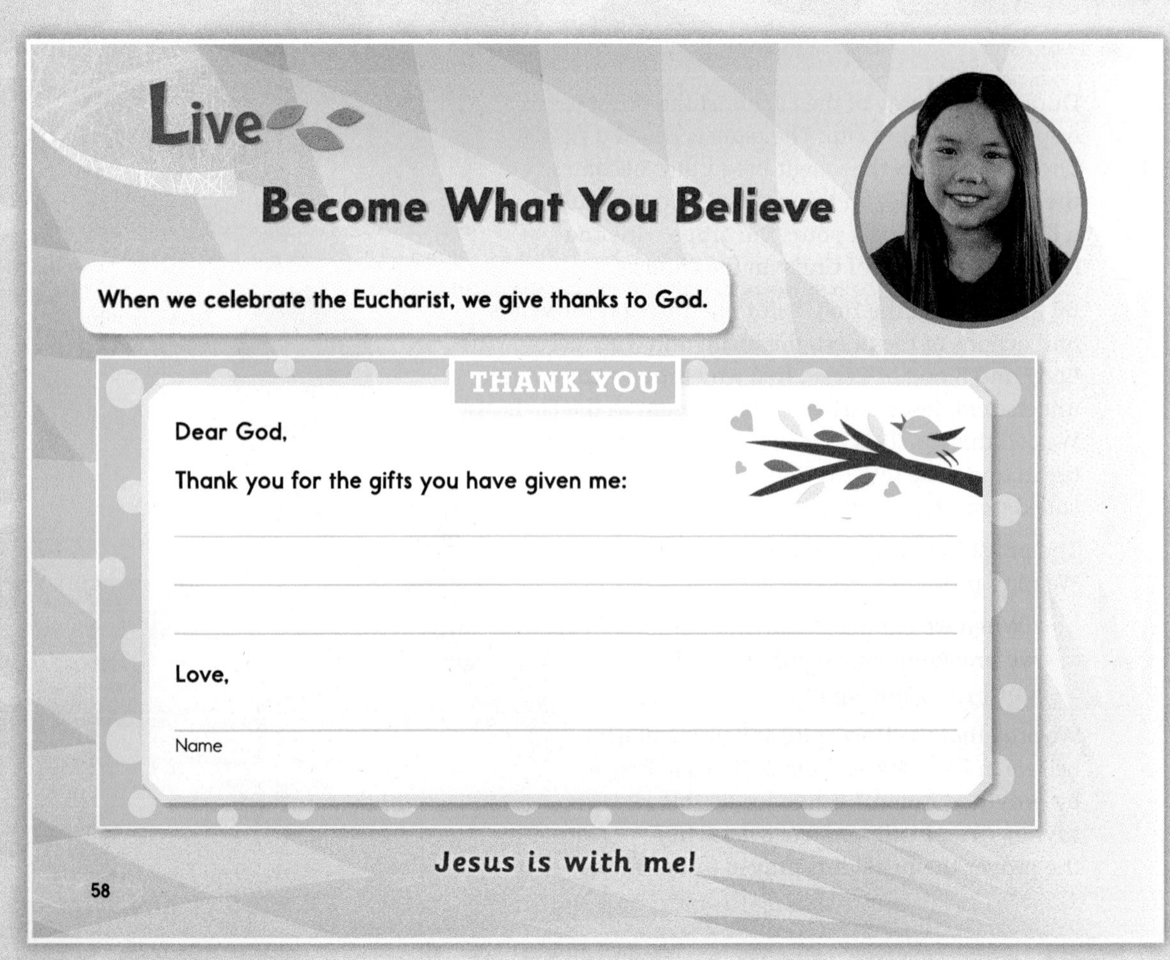

Live
Become What You Believe
When we celebrate the Eucharist, we give thanks to God.
THANK YOU
Dear God,
Thank you for the gifts you have given me:
Love,
Name
Jesus is with me!
58

Discipleship in Action

Read the story of Saint Brigid on page 59. Explain that Saint Brigid lived in Ireland. Point out Ireland on a world map, if available.

Explain through discussion ways Saint Brigid was kind to others as a child. Have the children share a few ways they can be kind and giving.

Activity

- Prepare the children for the "Discipleship in Action" activity. Have them think about ways that people have been kind to them and how kindness made them feel.
- Explain that God works through us. All acts of kindness help others experience the love of God.
- Have the children complete the "Discipleship in Action" activity. Invite them to share their responses with the group.

Celebrating Cultural Diversity

Traditions and customs from cultures that make up our one Church

The Feast of Corpus Christi celebrates the Real Presence of Christ in the Eucharist. In Poland the holy day is known as *Boże Ciało*. It is marked with elaborate processions that begin at churches in villages and cities throughout the country. Following the celebration of Mass, the priest walks through the streets carrying the Blessed Sacrament. Girls in white Communion dresses walk in front of the Blessed Sacrament, scattering rose petals or other flowers to honor Christ's presence. The procession stops at four altars along the route to read a passage from one of the four Gospels.

Discipleship in Action

Saint Brigid (A.D. 453–523)

Saint Brigid was the daughter of an Irish king. From a young age she was known for her kind and giving ways. She would give food and clothing to the poor. She even sometimes gave away things that belonged to her father, the king! When Brigid grew up she became a nun. Saint Brigid started the first religious community of women in Ireland. She helped to build many convents and schools all over Ireland. Saint Brigid was known for sharing peace and kindness with everyone she met.

I can show kindness to someone in need by . . .

Live

Our God Is Here

Read and familiarize yourself with the prayer and the music selection. To prepare the environment, arrange the following items on a small table:

- white tablecloth
- glass bowl half full of holy water
- baptismal candle in holder near bowl
- Bible on a table stand

You will also need:

- CD player
- Music CD, queued to play track "Our God Is Here"

Invite the children to gather around the table with their books. Teach them the song "Our God Is Here." Ask the children to quiet themselves for prayer.

Invite the children to bless themselves with holy water at the opening of the prayer. Briefly describe this ritual action and ask the children to follow your lead when you go to bless yourself with holy water. Pray the prayer together, ending with the Lord's Prayer (page 93 of child's book).

Conclude the prayer ritual with the following "mystagogy," or reflection on the experience. Invite the children to give one- or two-word responses to the following:

- *How do you feel when you proclaim "Our God is here"?*
- *What words from the song do you remember most?*
- *What does it mean to you to be Jesus' light in the world?*

Notes ______________________

____

____

Our God Is Here

All: (*Listen to verse one.*)
Here in this time, here in this place, here we are standing face to face. . . .

(*Refrain*) And we cry: "Holy, Holy, Holy are you!"

We cry: "Holy, Holy, Holy and true!"

Amen, we do believe our God is here.

Our God is here.

Leader: God is here with us now, and in a special way in the Body and Blood of Jesus. Each time we go to Mass and receive Holy Communion, we celebrate the love of God in Jesus.

All: (*Listen to verse two.*)

Here in the Word, God is revealed, here where the wounded can be healed. . . .

(*Sing refrain.*)

Leader: Lord Jesus, you are alive in our hearts. Help us to bring your love to our families, and to our friends and neighbors in the world. Help us to be your light in the world. Let us join hands and pray as Jesus taught us.

All: Our Father . . .

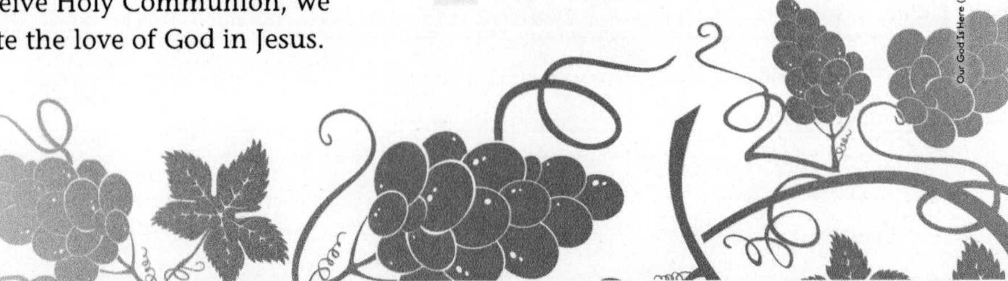

Living Faith at Home

Encourage family participation by having the children take home the double-sided "Living Faith at Home" page.

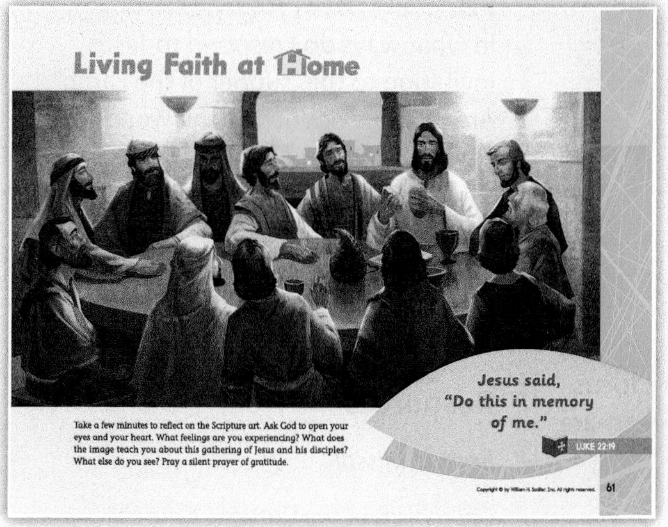

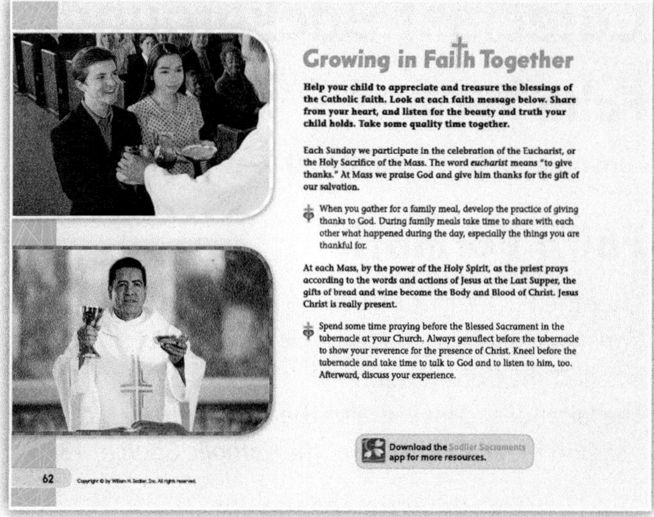

Celebrating Inclusion

Strategies and tips for including children with disabilities

Use the following tips to teach this chapter through a multisensory approach, which may benefit not only children with learning differences but others as well. The more we teach in a multisensory approach that includes auditory, visual, and tactile-kinesthetic (hands-on) opportunities for learning, the more learners we will reach when we teach.

Believe Allow children who lack writing skills to draw pictures or respond verbally on page 50.

For visual learners, draw extra attention to the photos of giving and receiving gifts on page 51. Offer a detailed description of each photo. For hands-on learners, give each child an envelope wrapped in ribbon with a holy card inside. Discuss how it felt to receive the gift.

Celebrate On page 54, have unconsecrated hosts and wine available for visual learners to see what is being discussed. Display a picture of the altar in the parish church if a visit there is not possible.

To help children with page 57, invite a priest or deacon to display the sacred vessels he uses at Mass, such as the paten and chalice, demonstrating reverence for them.

Live On page 58, allow the children to respond verbally or to choose from a selection of pictures that depict gifts that come from God. This will benefit visual learners. Auditory learners will benefit from having the pictures described.

On page 59, allow children who lack writing skills to respond verbally or by drawing a picture.

On page 60, have the children prepare strips of paper that include the words "Holy, Holy, Holy are you!" to be waved as the refrain to the song is sung, promoting engagement of visual and hands-on learners. During the Lord's Prayer, allow children who are sensitive to touch to raise their uplifted palms instead of holding hands.

Notes

Receiving the Body and Blood of Christ

Catechist Background

Faith Focus

I am blessed to be called to the Lord's Supper.

Faith Formation

After the Eucharistic Prayer, we prepare for and then receive Jesus Christ in Holy Communion. This part of the Liturgy of the Eucharist is called the Communion Rite. The altar continues to be the focus. The "altar of sacrifice" is also the "table of the Lord" where we share a sacred meal (*Catechism of the Catholic Church*, 1383).

Christ himself invites the community to gather at his altar to share in his own Body and Blood, sacrificed for all. He extends his invitation through the priest who prays, "Blessed are those called to the supper of the Lamb" *(Roman Missal)*. When we respond to Christ's invitation, we receive the greatest gift of love—Jesus, the Bread of Life.

To begin the Communion Rite, we stand in unity to pray the Lord's Prayer. We then exchange a sign of peace. This gesture shows that we are the Body of Christ, united to Jesus Christ and to one another. The priest then breaks the consecrated Host, now the Body of Christ. All those who gather at the Table of the Lord share the one Bread of Life.

As the Communion Rite continues, we join in song as we go forward to receive Holy Communion. This is yet another expression of our unity and joy as members of Christ's Body, the Church. Once the Communion hymn has ended, we offer our own prayer of thanksgiving in silence.

As you present this chapter, help the children to understand that it is Jesus who invites us to receive Holy Communion. When we receive Christ's own Body and Blood, Jesus Christ unites us to himself and to one another as the Body of Christ.

For Personal Reflection

In what ways do I respond to Jesus' invitation to the "supper of the Lamb"? Are my eyes opened to the wonder of Jesus' great gift of love?

Catechist Prayer

Risen Lord, you give us the gift of yourself in the Eucharist. Unite us in your love and bring us your peace.

Resources

Roman Missal

Catechism of the Catholic Church, 1088, 1382–1390

We Believe, Catholic Identity Edition, Grade 2, Chapter 18

Believe—Celebrate—Live: Eucharist DVD, Chapter 5 video; Music CD, "*Pan de Vida*"

Celebrating Inclusion

Strategies and tips for including children with disabilities are found on page 75–76.

Words of Faith

Holy Communion

sign of peace

Host

Introduce the Chapter

Review the lesson introduction on page 63.

 Play the video segment introducing the chapter. Alternatively, share the story below.

Read-Aloud Story (Optional)

Michael

Soon I will be receiving Jesus in Holy Communion. I know that Jesus is the Son of God. He died and rose again for me and for all people. Jesus Christ invites me to receive him in the Eucharist and to grow as his disciple. This is so exciting for me!

I like that we walk with our hands folded in prayer in procession to receive Holy Communion. It helps me to remember that we are sharing this meal together. And we sing together, too! My parish family usually sings a hymn about the Body and Blood of Christ that we share.

I will remember to bow my head before receiving the Body of Christ and then again before receiving the Blood of Christ from the chalice. I know that I will be receiving an awesome gift: Jesus Christ himself! Jesus is really present in the Sacrament of the Eucharist.

- **What do you think I will say and do after I receive Holy Communion?**

Receiving the Body and Blood of Christ

Chapter Planner

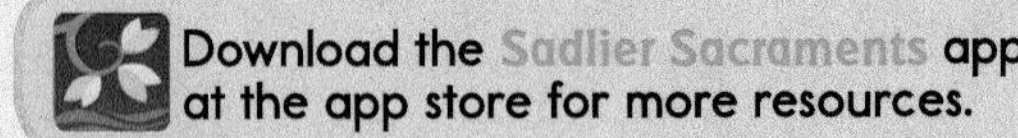

Time	Materials	Steps
Believe pages 64–67		
15–20 minutes	• battery-operated candle • Chapter 5 video • crayons or colored pencils • Bible open to the Scripture passage on page 66, for direct reading of the Scripture	• Pray the words from the *Roman Missal*. • View and discuss the Chapter 5 video (or share the Read-Aloud Story, page 63B). • Complete the activity about a celebration. • Read and discuss the text. • Discuss the photograph. • Complete the prayer-writing activity. • Read aloud the Scripture story of Jesus on the Road to Emmaus, and engage in the *Lectio* and *Visio Divina* exercise.
Celebrate pages 68–71		
20–30 minutes	• unconsecrated hosts or small pieces of pita bread, and a cup or cruet of water	• Present the text and complete the activities. • Present the "Catholic Identity" and "Catholic Faith and Life" features. • Discuss the photographs. • Discuss the Words of Faith. • Present the "Celebrating Cultural Diversity" feature.
Live pages 72–74		
10–15 minutes	• prayer space materials listed on page 74 • *Believe—Celebrate—Live* Music CD	• Prepare the prayer space. • Discuss what it means to be invited to the Lord's Supper. • Complete the activity. • Read and respond to the "Discipleship in Action" story and activity. • Pray and sing "Bread of Life/*Pan de Vida.*" • Close with reflection questions. • Remind the children to bring home the "Living Faith at Home" page.

Key: Prayer | Video | Scripture | Pray and Sing

Introduce the Chapter

Receiving the Body and Blood of Christ

Welcome the children. Tell them that they will be learning about receiving the gift of Jesus Christ himself in Holy Communion.

Gather for prayer. Light a battery-operated candle. Then pray together the Sign of the Cross. Call attention to the prayer on page 63, from the *Roman Missal*. Pray this blessing together.

Share that the priest prays these words before we receive Holy Communion. The priest invites us to receive the Body and Blood of Christ.

Introduce the video segment for this chapter by saying, "Let's explore some of the themes of this chapter with our young friends from the chapter video." Play the video.

Alternatively, you may choose to share the Read-Aloud Story found on page 63B of this guide.

Notes

Receiving the Body and Blood of Christ
CHAPTER
5
"Blessed are those called to the supper of the Lamb."
—Roman Missal
63

Believe

Open Your Heart

Ask the children the following or similar questions about what they saw in the video or heard in the Read-Aloud Story:

What do we believe about Jesus in Holy Communion?

What do we do before receiving Holy Communion to show that we believe Jesus is really present in the consecrated Bread and Wine?

What did you see or hear that was different or new to you?

Notes ______________________________

____

____

____

Activity

- Ask the children to imagine that they are with family or friends at their favorite celebration. What is the celebration for? Who is there? What does everyone do together?
- Discuss some of the reasons why we have celebrations. Talk about some of the things families do at special meal celebrations. Examples might include lighting candles, singing songs, telling favorite family stories, praying, and sharing favorite foods.
- Distribute crayons or colored pencils. Invite the children to complete the activity.
- Encourage the children to share with a partner their one-word description of how they feel at the celebration.

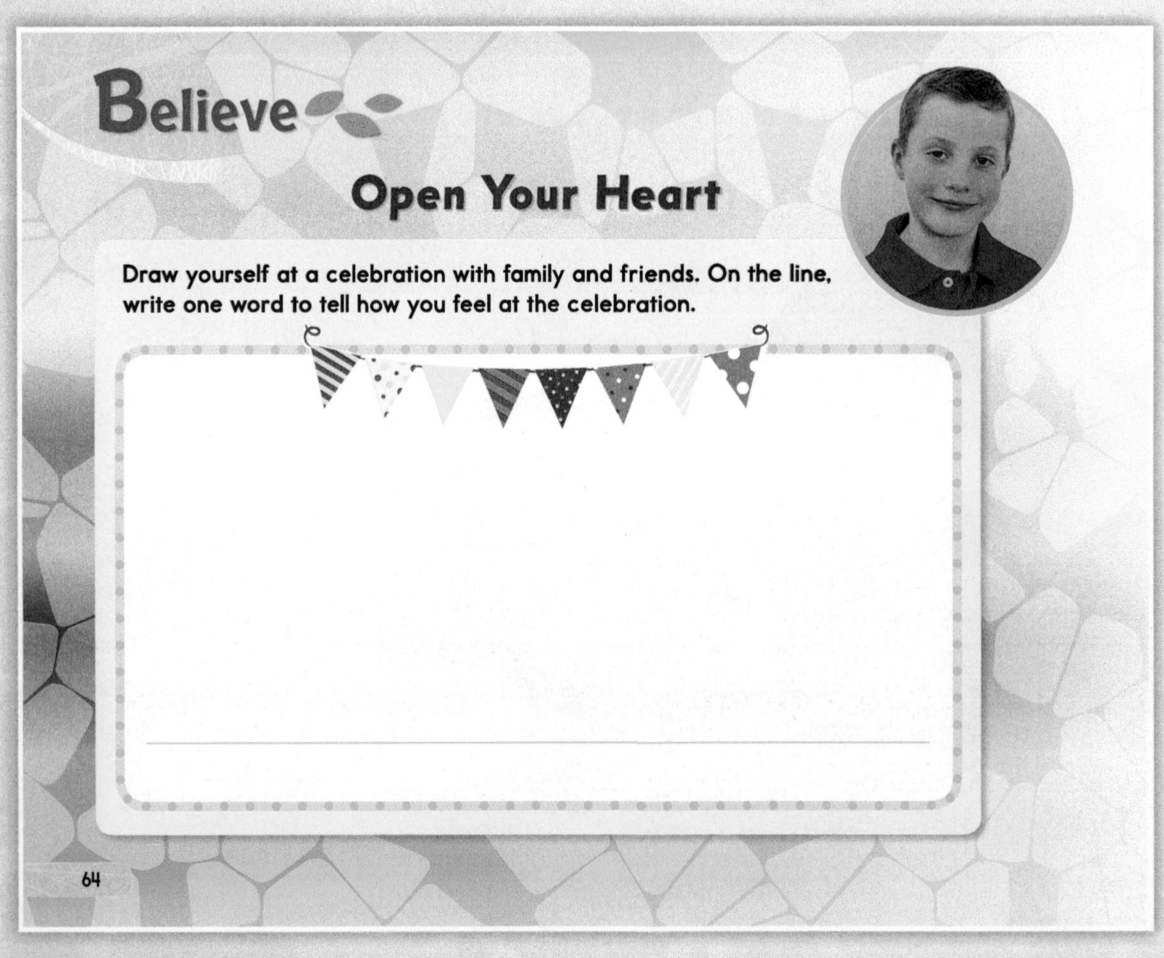

Believe
Open Your Heart
Draw yourself at a celebration with family and friends. On the line, write one word to tell how you feel at the celebration.
64

A Special Invitation

Share with the children some of the reasons you celebrate with others. Invite them to share some of their reasons.

Read aloud the first paragraph.

Ask *What is it like to be invited to a celebration?*

Read the last paragraph. Ask what is happening in the photograph. (Families may be greeting the priest before or after the celebration of the Eucharist.)

Ask *How are our family celebrations similar to or different from the celebration of the Eucharist?* Help the children conclude that both celebrations are gatherings of people who share love and joy. But the Eucharist is different from any other celebration. At Mass we gather as the Body of Christ to remember Jesus' Death and Resurrection. We remember who we are as the baptized by receiving the gift of Jesus, the Bread of Life, in Holy Communion.

Read the quotation from John's Gospel together. Ask the children what they think Jesus meant by this. Explain that Jesus, who is the Bread of Life, helps us to live in God's love now and forever.

Activity

- Work with the children to write a prayer to Jesus. Write the following on chart paper: *Jesus, Bread of Life, help us to be…*
- Have the children quietly think about how Jesus wants us to live. Then invite them to think of one word, such as *understanding* or *giving*, to complete the prayer. List their responses on the chart paper.
- Pray the prayer together.

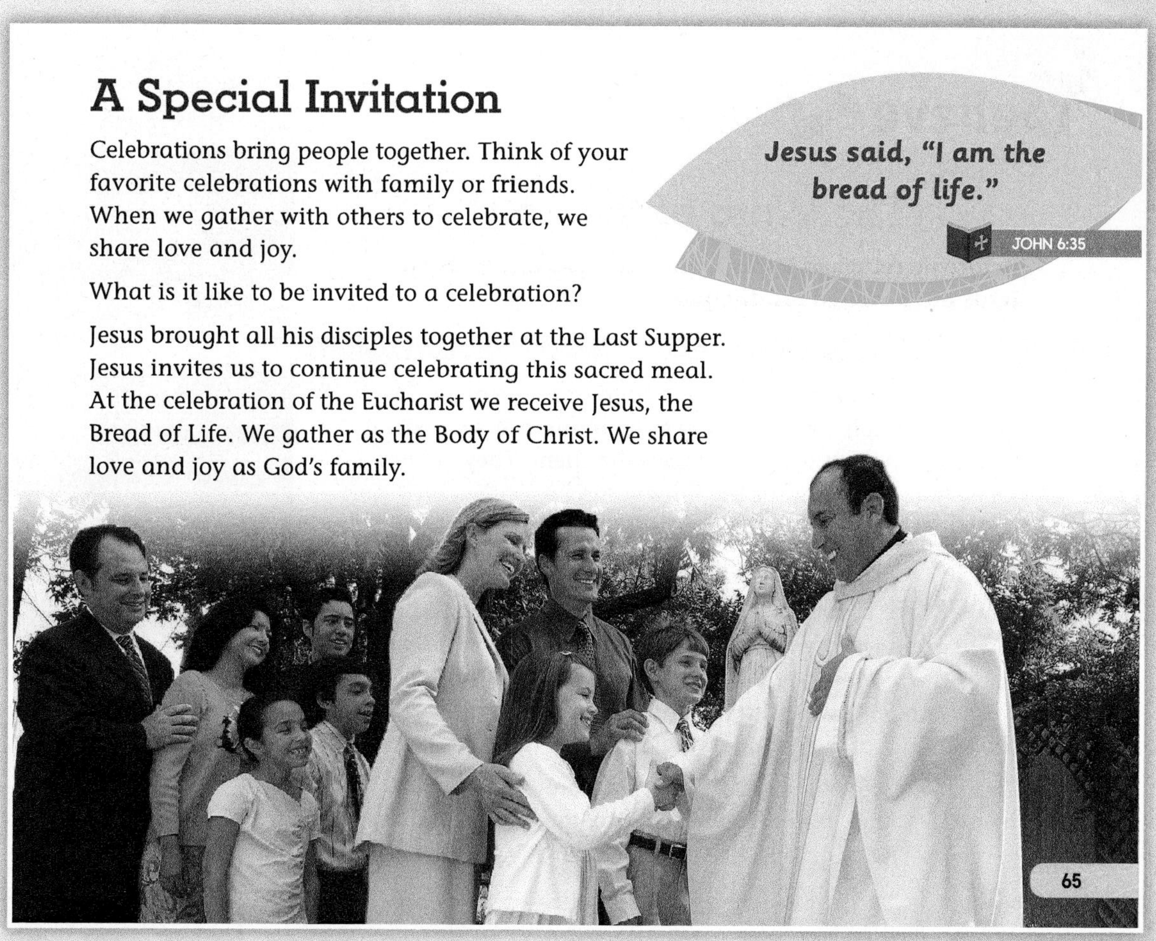

A Special Invitation

Celebrations bring people together. Think of your favorite celebrations with family or friends. When we gather with others to celebrate, we share love and joy.

What is it like to be invited to a celebration?

Jesus brought all his disciples together at the Last Supper. Jesus invites us to continue celebrating this sacred meal. At the celebration of the Eucharist we receive Jesus, the Bread of Life. We gather as the Body of Christ. We share love and joy as God's family.

Jesus said, "I am the bread of life."

JOHN 6:35

65

Believe

The Word of the Lord

Share with the children that before the Risen Jesus returned to his Father in heaven, he visited his disciples several times. On some of those occasions, Jesus shared a meal with his followers. Say: *The story you will read today is a story about one of those visits.*

Read aloud the introductory paragraph before the Scripture. This will help reinforce the essential background information.

Explain that the children are going to hear a reading from the Bible, the living Word of God. This is a reading from the Gospel of Luke.

Guide the children through an adaptation of *Lectio Divina*, a special way to pray with Scripture. Quiet the children, and ask them to listen carefully to the Scripture reading as you read it aloud.

Reflect on the reading by inviting the children to:

- Take a moment to think about what they heard.
- Silently answer the following questions for reflection (be sure to pause after each question): *What word or words did you hear? What do you think Jesus is saying to you?*
- Quietly hold these words in their hearts. (Pause in prayer.)
- Share aloud in one or two words what they heard. Describe what they were feeling in their hearts. (Accept all responses.)

Guide the children through an adaptation of *Visio Divina*, a special way to pray with Scripture art. Quiet the children, and invite them to take their time looking at the illustration on pages 66 and 67. Read aloud the Scripture once again. Invite the children to silently answer these questions: *What do you see? What does it mean to you? What do you imagine Jesus inviting you to see? What do you think this means for you?*

The Word of the Lord

Before he returned to his Father in heaven, the Risen Jesus often visited his disciples.

Based on LUKE 24:13–35

It was the Sunday that Jesus had risen from the dead. Two of Jesus' disciples were walking to Emmaus, a town near Jerusalem. A man started walking with them. They did not know that this man was the Risen Jesus.

The disciples talked to the man about what had happened the past three days: Jesus was crucified, died, and was buried. And now his body was missing from the tomb.

It was getting dark when they reached the town. The disciples asked the man to stay. He did, and joined them for a meal. Then, "while he was with them at table, he took bread, said the blessing, broke it, and gave it to them" (Luke 24:30).

Then the disciples recognized that this man was the Risen Jesus. They knew him "in the breaking of the bread" (Luke 24:35).

66

Share After the silent reflection, allow time for sharing aloud responses to these questions. Then invite the children to look again at the picture and silently answer the questions *What are some things this picture tells you about our journey with Jesus? What does it tell you about how we know that Jesus is with us?* Invite volunteers to share their responses aloud.

Check comprehension by asking the following questions:

What were the two disciples talking about on the road to Emmaus? (They were talking about Jesus, who had been crucified, died, and was buried.)

While they were talking, who joined them? (Jesus joined them, but they did not recognize him.)

What did Jesus do that helped his disciples to recognize him? (At the meal he took bread, said the blessing, broke the bread, and gave it to his disciples, just as he had done at the Last Supper.)

Scripture Background

On Sunday, three days after he suffered and died on the Cross, Jesus Christ rose from the dead. On the road to Emmaus, the Risen Jesus appeared to his disciples, and he shared a meal with them, in the same way he did at the Last Supper. In the breaking of the bread, the disciples came to know that it was Jesus who was truly with them. When we gather together to celebrate the Eucharist, we also recognize the Risen Jesus in the "breaking of the bread."

Notes ______________________

____

____

____

Celebrate

Preparing for Holy Communion

Invite the children to recall the parts of the Liturgy of the Eucharist from Chapter 4. Stress that during the Eucharistic Prayer, through the power of the Holy Spirit and the words and actions of the priest, the bread and wine become the Body and Blood of Christ. Explain that today we will be talking about the last part of the Liturgy of the Eucharist—the Communion Rite.

Read aloud the first paragraph on page 68. Explain that we prepare to receive Jesus in Holy Communion by praying together the prayer Jesus taught us.

Ask *What is another name for this prayer?* (the Lord's Prayer) *What do we prepare to do after the Eucharistic Prayer?* (We prepare to receive Jesus himself in Holy Communion.)

Direct attention to the photo of people sharing a sign of peace. Then read aloud the last paragraph on page 68. Stress that we should share the sign of peace in a prayerful and respectful way. The gift of peace that we share with one another comes from Christ.

Celebrating Cultural Diversity

Traditions and customs from cultures that make up our one Church

A Catholic Mass celebrated in Vietnam reflects some of the beautiful customs of the culture. For example, before exchanging a sign of peace, the assembly first bows to the priest. Most distinctive in the liturgy is the chanting of prayers or sacred text, known as *doc kinh*. Vietnamese chanting at Mass is a beautiful blend of tones and sounds, which are different from singing a hymn. The repetition of chanting helps the children to remember their prayers.

Celebrate

Preparing for Holy Communion

In the Liturgy of the Eucharist, after the Eucharistic Prayer, we prepare to receive Jesus himself in the Eucharist. Through the power of the Holy Spirit and the action of the priest, our gifts of bread and wine have now become the Body and Blood of Christ. And we will receive the Body and Blood of Christ in **Holy Communion**. Like the disciples at Emmaus, we recognize Jesus "in the breaking of the bread."

We join ourselves with the whole Church as we pray aloud or sing the Lord's Prayer. Then the priest reminds us of Jesus' words at the Last Supper. Jesus said, "Peace I leave with you; my peace I give to you" (John 14:27).

We share the gift of Christ's peace with one another.

Direct attention to the photo of the priest breaking the large Host on page 69. Explain that while the priest is breaking the Host, we join with him in praying to Jesus Christ, the Lamb of God. The Eucharist is the center of our lives as Catholics.

Read aloud the text on page 69.

Check comprehension by asking these questions:

Why do we share a sign of peace? (to show that we are united to Jesus Christ and one another)

What does the priest do as we pray the "Lamb of God"? (The priest breaks the Host, the Bread that has become the Body of Christ.)

Activity

Practice the prayers and gestures presented on pages 68 and 69. Pray the Lord's Prayer together, greet one another with a sign of peace, and pray the words of the "Lamb of God."

Words of Faith

Holy Communion (page 68)
sign of peace (page 69)
Host (page 69)

CATHOLIC IDENTITY

Read aloud the statement on page 69. Pray together: *Thank you, Jesus, for inviting us to receive your Body and Blood. May we always welcome you into our hearts.*

Notes

We pray that Christ's peace may be with us always. We share a **sign of peace** with the people who are near us. When we do this we show that we are united to the Risen Lord, Jesus Christ, and to one another as the Body of Christ.

After we share a sign of peace, we pray to Jesus, who sacrificed his life to save us from sin. We ask him for forgiveness and peace. We begin the prayer with these words:

> "Lamb of God, you take away
> the sins of the world,
> have mercy on us."

As we pray the Lamb of God, the priest breaks the **Host**, the Bread that has become the Body of Christ. The priest puts a small piece in the chalice as a sign of the unity of the Body and Blood of Jesus Christ.

CATHOLIC IDENTITY

When we receive Holy Communion, we are receiving Jesus Christ himself.

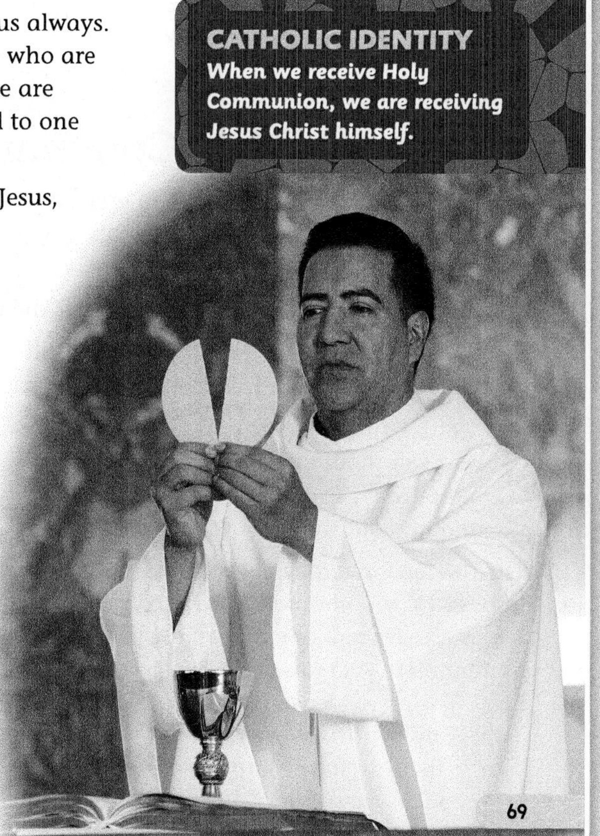

Like Jesus at the Last Supper, the priest breaks the Bread that has become the Body of Christ.

Celebrate

Receiving Holy Communion

Read aloud the first paragraph on page 70. Ask: *Who is the Lamb of God?* (Jesus)

Explain that "Blessed are those called to the supper of the Lamb" is the same prayer the children prayed at the beginning of this chapter. Explain that it is Jesus who invites us to receive his Body and Blood. He does this through these words.

Read aloud our response to Jesus' invitation in the second paragraph. Remind the children that when we receive the Body and Blood of Christ in Holy Communion we are receiving the greatest gift of love. Our response shows that we want to receive Jesus into our hearts.

Read aloud the final paragraph. Explain that walking forward to receive Jesus in Holy Communion is called the Communion Procession. Explain that we go forward with our hands folded in prayer.

Direct attention to the photographs on pages 70 and 71 that show the proper way to receive Holy Communion. Emphasize that the Body and Blood of Christ are truly present in both the consecrated Bread and the consecrated Wine. Allow time to study and talk about each photograph. Explain that it is each person's choice whether to receive the Host in the hand or on the tongue, and whether to receive from the chalice.

Notes ______________________________

____

____

____

____

Celebrate

Receiving Holy Communion

After we pray the Lamb of God, the priest invites us to receive Jesus Christ in Holy Communion. The priest prays,

"Behold the Lamb of God,
behold him who takes away the sins of the world.
Blessed are those called to the supper of the Lamb."

Together with the priest we pray,

"Lord, I am not worthy
that you should enter under my roof,
but only say the word
and my soul shall be healed."

Then we go forward with reverence and love to receive Jesus in Holy Communion. Each of us stands before the priest, deacon, or extraordinary minister of Holy Communion, who raises the Host before us. We bow our head. The priest, deacon, or extraordinary minister says, "The Body of Christ." We respond, "Amen," and then receive the Host in the hand or on the tongue.

We bow our head before receiving the Host, the Body of Christ.

Read aloud the text on page 71.

Check comprehension by asking: *What is the first thing we do when we approach the priest, deacon, or extraordinary minister to receive Holy Communion?* (We bow our heads.) *What response do we say when we hear "the Body of Christ"?* (We say, "Amen.") *What response do we say when we hear "the Blood of Christ"?* (We say, "Amen.")

Explain and emphasize the importance of joining in the singing of the hymn. Explain that singing together is a sign of unity and joy.

Invite the children to pray with you the "Prayer after Communion" on page 94. Say to the children: *Once the hymn is completed, you can say this prayer or pray in your own words to thank Jesus for the gift of himself in Holy Communion.*

Catholic Faith and Life

Direct attention to the feature on the meaning of our "Amen" response before we receive the Body of Christ and the Blood of Christ. Explain that when we say "Amen," we express our faith.

Activity

- Practice the gestures and responses for receiving Holy Communion. Use unconsecrated hosts or small pieces of pita bread and a cup or cruet of water. Make sure that you emphasize that the hosts are unconsecrated.
- Refer to pages 91 and 92 in the child's text to help you demonstrate the proper way to receive Holy Communion.

Notes ____________________

____

Jesus is offering his very self to us in Holy Communion. When we respond, "Amen," we show that we believe Jesus is really present. We welcome Jesus with open hearts.

If we are also receiving from the chalice, the priest, deacon, or extraordinary minister of Holy Communion raises the chalice. Again, we bow our head. The priest, deacon, or extraordinary minister says, "The Blood of Christ." We respond, "Amen," and then drink from the cup.

As the gathered assembly joins in procession and receives the Body and Blood of Christ, we sing a hymn to express our unity. We are united with the whole Church, the Body of Christ.

After everyone has received Holy Communion there is usually some time for quiet prayer. During this time we remember that Jesus is present within us. We thank Jesus for the gift of himself in Holy Communion.

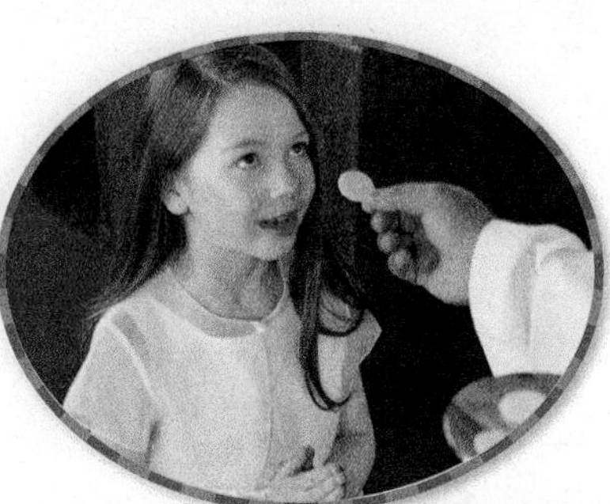

We may choose to receive the Host, the Body of Christ, on our tongue.

When we drink from the chalice in Holy Communion, we receive the Blood of Christ.

Become What You Believe

Invite the children to talk about why the celebration of the Eucharist, the Mass, is such a special celebration.

Direct the discussion to a synopsis of the Mass by putting an image on the board to represent each of the following: (1) cross, (2) altar, (3) host and chalice. As you point to each image, read aloud its corresponding statement:
(1) *Jesus Christ is the Lamb of God who takes away the sins of the world.*

(2) *We gather around the altar as the Body of Christ. We share love and joy.*

(3) *Jesus himself invites us to the Lord's Supper to receive his own Body and Blood. We believe that Jesus, the Son of God, is really present!*

Direct the children's attention to the statement in bold at the bottom of the page. Ask the group to read it aloud together and to think about what it means in their lives.

Activity

- Read aloud the directions for the activity on inviting someone to attend Mass. Direct attention to each part of the invitation.
- Recall with the children that the celebration of the Eucharist on the Lord's Day (Sunday) takes place on Saturday evening or on Sunday. They may write the time that their family usually attends Mass.
- Encourage the children to share the invitation with the person they are inviting.

Notes ______________________________

____

Live

Become What You Believe

Invite someone special to attend Mass. Complete the invitation below.

To: ______________________________

You are invited to ______________________________

Day and time: ______________________________

Place: ______________________________

Prepare for this celebration by ______________________________

____

____

____

____

I am blessed to be called to the Lord's Supper.

72

Discipleship in Action

Read the story of Saint Josephine Bakhita on page 73. Introduce the story by sharing a map of Sudan, in Africa, the place where Josephine Bakhita lived as a child.

Explain that even though Josephine was born into slavery, which led to a difficult life, she always knew that God was with her. Ask: *How do you know that God is with you?*

Reflect on the people who helped Josephine grow in her love for God. Share that we also have people in our lives who help us to see God's goodness and love.

Invite the children to share with the group the people who *first* helped them to know and follow Jesus Christ.

Activity

- Share that there are many people who help to bring us closer to Jesus and live as his disciples. Some may teach us about our Catholic faith. Others may show us by their example how to follow Jesus Christ.
- Have the children think about who has helped them, then have them complete the activity.

Notes

Discipleship in Action

Saint Josephine Bakhita (1869–1957)

As a child, Josephine Bakhita lived as a slave in Sudan, in Africa. Her life was very difficult, but she still saw beauty in the world around her. In her heart, Josephine longed to know God. Eventually she came to live with kind and caring nuns in Italy, where she gained her freedom. The nuns helped Josephine to see God's goodness and love. They taught her to become a follower of Jesus Christ and prepare for Baptism. And they welcomed her when she was called by God to join their religious community. Josephine was a joyful nun. She was happy to help others experience God's love and peace. *Bakhita* means "fortunate one."

I thank God for all the people who help me to follow Jesus Christ, including . . .

Live 

Bread of Life/*Pan de Vida* 

Read and familiarize yourself with the prayer and the music selection. To prepare the environment, arrange the following items on a small table:

- white tablecloth
- crucifix
- baptismal candle in holder
- Bible on a table stand
- cup or goblet that resembles a chalice (optional)
- unconsecrated host, or a loaf of bread (optional)

You will also need:

- CD player
- Music CD queued to play the track "*Pan de Vida*"

Invite the children to gather around the table with their books. Teach them the song "*Pan de Vida.*" Ask the children to quiet themselves for prayer. Briefly describe the ritual action in the prayer—sharing a sign of peace while saying "Peace be with you." Pray the prayer together, ending with the sign of peace.

Conclude the prayer ritual with the following "mystagogy," or reflection on the experience. Invite the children to give one- or two-word responses to the following:

- *What words from the song or the prayer do you remember most?*
- *What do you think "at this table the last shall be first" means?*
- *How did it feel to share a sign of peace?*

Notes ______________________________

____

Live 

Bread of Life/*Pan de Vida* 

All: (*Refrain*) *Pan de Vida, cuerpo del Señor,*
cup of blessing, blood of Christ the Lord.
At this table the last shall be first.
Poder es servir, porque Dios es amor.

Leader: We receive the Body of Christ, the Bread of Life.
We drink of the cup of blessing, the Blood of Christ the Lord.

When we receive Holy Communion, we receive the Body of Christ, the Bread of Life. We bring the peace of Christ to those we love and to the world.

All: (*Refrain*)

Leader: This sacred meal that we will share is given to us so that we may share the love of Jesus in the world. We are blessed to be called to the Table of the Lord.

All: (*Refrain*)

Leader: When we eat this bread and drink this cup we proclaim the Death of the Lord, until he comes again.

All: (*Refrain*)

Leader: The peace of the Lord is with us, and we are to share Christ's peace with others. Let us offer one another a sign of peace.

Living Faith at Home

Encourage family participation by having the children take home the double-sided "Living Faith at Home" page.

Living Faith at Home

Jesus "was made known to them in the breaking of the bread."

LUKE 24:35

Take a few minutes to reflect on the Scripture art. Ask God to open your eyes and your heart. What feelings are you experiencing? What are the people doing? Imagine yourself in the scene. What are you thinking? What else do you see? Pray a silent prayer of gratitude.

Copyright © by William H. Sadlier, Inc. All rights reserved. 75

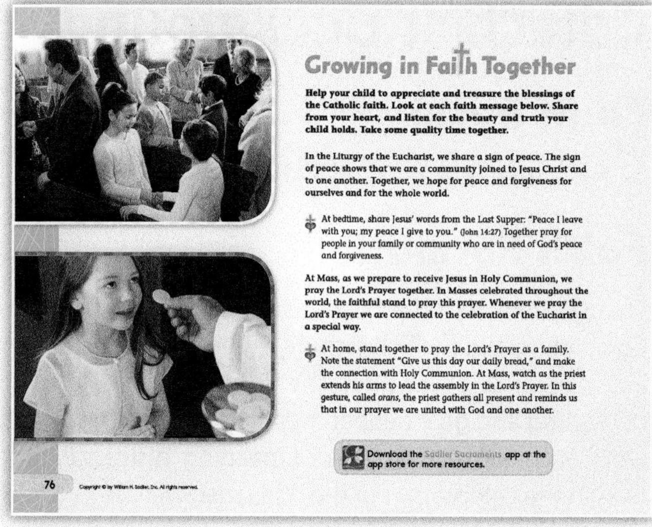

Growing in Faith Together

Help your child to appreciate and treasure the blessings of the Catholic faith. Look at each faith message below. Share from your heart, and listen for the beauty and truth your child holds. Take some quality time together.

In the Liturgy of the Eucharist, we share a sign of peace. The sign of peace shows that we are a community joined to Jesus Christ and to one another. Together, we hope for peace and forgiveness for ourselves and for the whole world.

- At bedtime, share Jesus' words from the Last Supper: "Peace I leave with you; my peace I give to you." (John 14:27) Together pray for people in your family or community who are in need of God's peace and forgiveness.

At Mass, as we prepare to receive Jesus in Holy Communion, we pray the Lord's Prayer together. In Masses celebrated throughout the world, the faithful stand to pray this prayer. Whenever we pray the Lord's Prayer we are connected to the celebration of the Eucharist in a special way.

- At home, stand together to pray the Lord's Prayer as a family. Note the statement "Give us this day our daily bread," and make the connection with Holy Communion. At Mass, watch as the priest extends his arms to lead the assembly in the Lord's Prayer. In this gesture, called *orans*, the priest gathers all present and reminds us that in our prayer we are united with God and one another.

Download the Sadlier Sacraments app at the app store for more resources.

76 Copyright © by William H. Sadlier, Inc. All rights reserved.

Celebrating Inclusion

Strategies and tips for including children with disabilities

Use the following tips to teach this chapter through a multisensory approach, which may benefit not only children with learning differences but others as well. The more we teach in a multisensory approach that includes auditory, visual, and tactile-kinesthetic (hands-on) opportunities for learning, the more learners we will reach when we teach.

Believe On page 64, allow children who lack fine motor skills to respond verbally or to choose from a selection of pictures depicting emotions.

On page 65, kinesthetic-tactile learners will enjoy acting out being invited to a celebration.

Celebrate On page 68, kinesthetic-tactile learners will benefit from sharing a sign of peace. For children who do not feel comfortable shaking hands, practice looking at someone and smiling as a way to share a sign of peace.

For pages 70 and 71, invite children who are visual and hands-on learners to act out the steps for receiving Communion at Mass, using unconsecrated hosts and grape juice. Children with sensory processing disorders may be receptive only to receiving the smallest piece of a host. If even that is not possible, they can receive from the chalice alone. Your pastor may want to be advised of sensory processing differences during preparation and at Mass. Parents might be advised that children who taste real wine before First Communion may be less likely to spit it out or make faces during the actual sacrament.

For children who need gluten-free hosts, demonstrate how to receive the host from their personal pyxes. Practice receiving on the tongue for those whose families use that method.

Live For pages 72 and 73, children who lack writing skills may respond verbally. Have a partner assist children with intellectual or developmental delays in completing the activities. Partners may need to tell how one prepares (for example, by dressing up, being joyful, praying) or naming people who help the children follow Jesus (for example, parents, grandparents, or catechists).

On page 74, again provide an alternate form for the sign of peace for those who are touch-sensitive.

Living as the Body of Christ

Catechist Background

Faith Focus

As a disciple I am sent out to love and serve God and others.

Faith Formation

The Sacrament of the Eucharist, the Mass, ends with the Concluding Rites, which include a greeting and blessing, dismissal, and reverence of the altar. The Concluding Rites really mark a beginning and give deeper meaning to why we were there. The word *Mass* comes from a word meaning "dismissal," or "to send out." In the celebration of the Eucharist, we have been strengthened by the Word of God and have received Christ himself in Holy Communion. Now we are called to live as baptized members of the Body of Christ. The priest, acting in Christ's name, commissions us to carry on Jesus' work of bringing love, compassion, and forgiveness to the world. Each of us is sent forth in mission to live a life of charity and to proclaim the Gospel to all people. Pope Francis emphasized that we cannot allow our encounter with the Risen Lord to "remain locked up. . . . Faith is a flame that grows stronger the more it is shared and passed on" (Pope Francis, July 28, 2013).

The challenge of serving others in our communities and throughout the world may seem overwhelming. Jesus gave this same challenge to his first disciples when he said, "Go . . . and make disciples of all nations" (Matthew 28:19). We must remember that we do not carry on Jesus' work alone. Jesus is always with us, guiding us to serve others, especially those who are in need. We trust that we can do as Jesus asks because of his promise, "I am with you always" (Matthew 28:20).

Explore the importance of the Concluding Rites with the children. Share Pope Francis' words: *"Go, do not be afraid, and serve"* (July 28, 2013).

For Personal Reflection

In what ways does the Sacrament of the Eucharist transform my life? In what ways do I live out the Church's mission and bring Jesus' love and generosity to others?

Catechist Prayer

Risen Lord, help me to trust in your promise, "I am with you always" (Matthew 28:20). Guide me in carrying on your work in the world.

Resources

Roman Missal

Catechism of the Catholic Church, 1332, 1397, 1416

We Believe, Catholic Identity Edition, Grade 2, Chapter 19

Believe—Celebrate—Live: Eucharist DVD, Chapter 6 video; Music CD, "We Are the Body of Christ/*Somos el Cuerpo de Cristo*"

Celebrating Inclusion

Strategies and tips for including children with disabilities are found on page 89–90.

Words of Faith

- Concluding Rites
- blessing
- tabernacle
- Most Blessed Sacrament

Introduce the Chapter

Review the lesson introduction on page 77.

Play the video segment introducing the chapter. Alternatively, share the story below.

Read-Aloud Story (Optional)

Megan

At the end of every Mass, the priest sends us out on a mission. He may say: "Go in peace, glorifying the Lord by your life." That sounds like a hard thing to do. But I think I understand. Listen to my story:

It was a Saturday. I had exciting news to share with my friend Kate. My family was going on a trip. We would be leaving in a few days! Kate lives next door, so I rushed to tell her all about the trip. "We are going to visit my cousins," I blurted out. Then I went on and on about my cousins and how they lived near a big city.

I didn't notice at first, but when I stopped talking, I saw that Kate seemed very sad. "My grandma fell and broke her hip," she said slowly. "We're really worried about her."

I listened to Kate talk about her grandma. I think it made her feel better. Then I suggested that we make a card for her grandma. "Let's use my new paints to make something really special for her," I said.

- **What else can I do for my friend to be caring and loving like Jesus?**

Living as the Body of Christ

Chapter Planner

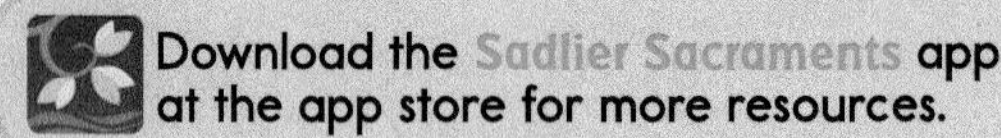

Time	Materials	Steps
Believe pages 78–81		
15–20 minutes	• battery-operated candle Chapter 6 video • drawing paper, colored pencils or crayons, large unlined index cards • Bible open to the Scripture passage on page 80, for direct reading of the Scripture	Pray the words from the *Roman Missal.* View and discuss the Chapter 6 video (or share the Read-Aloud Story, page 77B). • Read and discuss the text. • Discuss the photograph. • Complete the activity. Read aloud the Scripture story of the Commissioning of the Disciples, and engage in the *Lectio* and *Visio Divina* exercise.
Celebrate pages 82–85		
20–30 minutes		• Present the text. • Complete the activities. • Present the "Catholic Identity" and "Catholic Faith and Life" features. • Discuss the photographs and captions. • Discuss the Words of Faith. • Present the "Celebrating Cultural Diversity" feature.
Live pages 86–88		
10–15 minutes	• drawing paper and colored pencils or crayons for making posters about Jesus • prayer space materials listed on page 88 *Believe—Celebrate—Live* Music CD	• Prepare the prayer space. • Discuss ways to love and serve God and others. • Complete the activity. • Read and respond to the "Discipleship in Action" story and activity. Pray and sing "We Are the Body of Christ/*Somos el Cuerpo de Cristo.*" • Close with reflection questions. • Remind the children to bring home the "Living Faith at Home" page.

Key:  Prayer  Video  Scripture Pray and Sing

Introduce the Chapter

Living as the Body of Christ

Welcome the children and tell them that today they will hear about how Jesus helps us to share God's love with others.

Gather for prayer. Light a battery-operated candle. Then pray together the Sign of the Cross. Call attention to the prayer on page 77, from the *Roman Missal.* Proclaim the words together.

Share that the priest prays these words at the end of the Mass. We are sent out to serve God the Father, God the Son, and God the Holy Spirit by serving others.

Direct attention to the photograph of the family. Ask: *Why do you think the members of this family look happy?* Then, together, write a caption for the photograph. Tell the children that families can work together to care for others and the world around us.

Introduce the video segment for this chapter by saying, "Let's explore some of the themes of this chapter with our young friends from the chapter video." Play the video.

Alternatively, you may choose to share the Read-Aloud Story found on page 77B of this guide.

Notes ______________________________

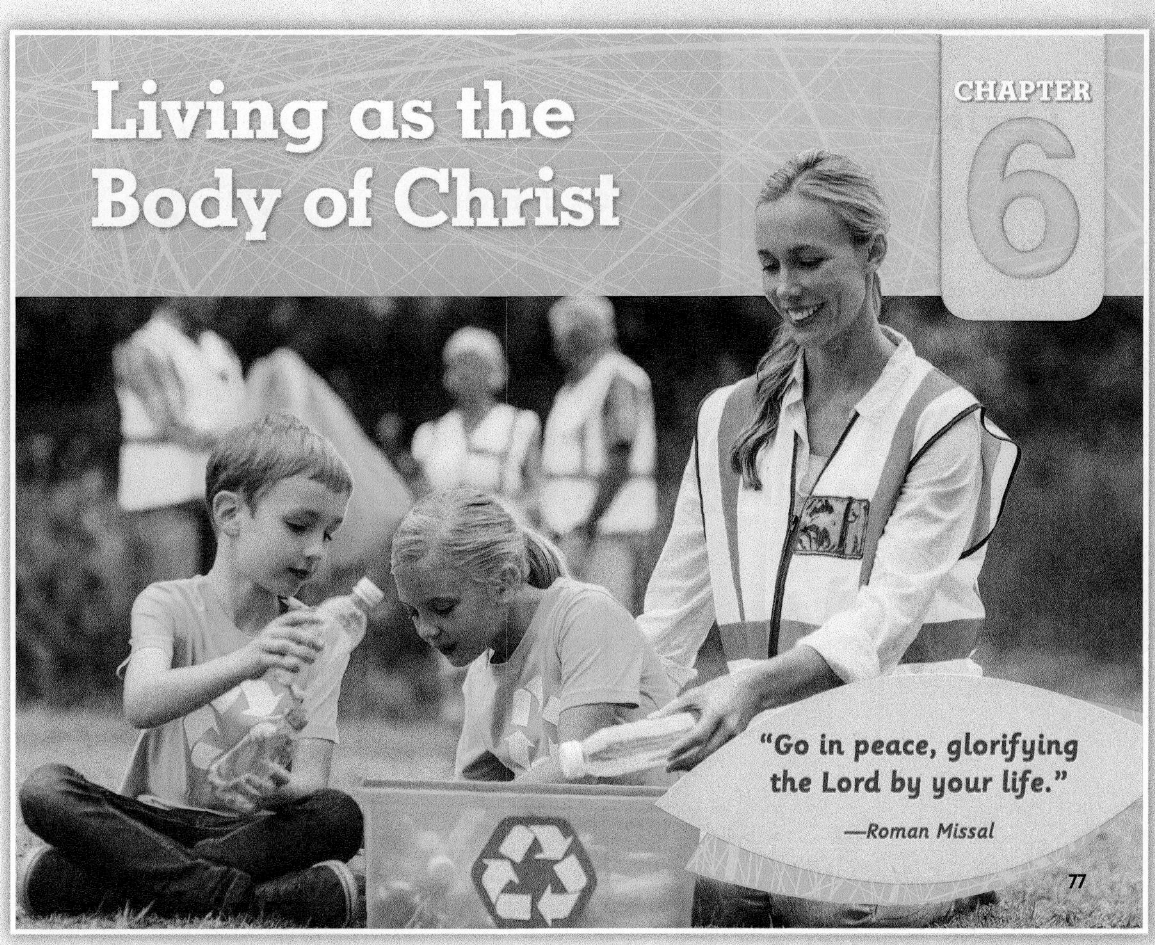

Living as the Body of Christ
CHAPTER 6
"Go in peace, glorifying the Lord by your life."
—Roman Missal
77

Believe

Open Your Heart

Ask the children the following or similar questions about what they saw in the video or heard in the Read-Aloud Story:

At the end of Mass, what does the priest send us forth to do?

What helps you to carry on the work of Jesus?

What did you see or hear that was different or new to you?

Invite the children to recall the photograph of the family on page 77. Share that families can work together to care for others and the world around us. Share your own experience of working together to care for others. Explain that there are many simple ways we can care for others and the world around us.

Share a few examples of situations where love and kindness are especially needed. Ask: *What kind words might you say to someone who is upset? sad?*

Activity

- Invite the children to complete the sentence starter "I show love and kindness to others . . ." They may write their kind actions and words in the smaller hearts. Then, in the center heart, have the children draw a picture of a kind and loving action they can do.
- Encourage the children to describe the loving action they drew in the center heart.

Notes

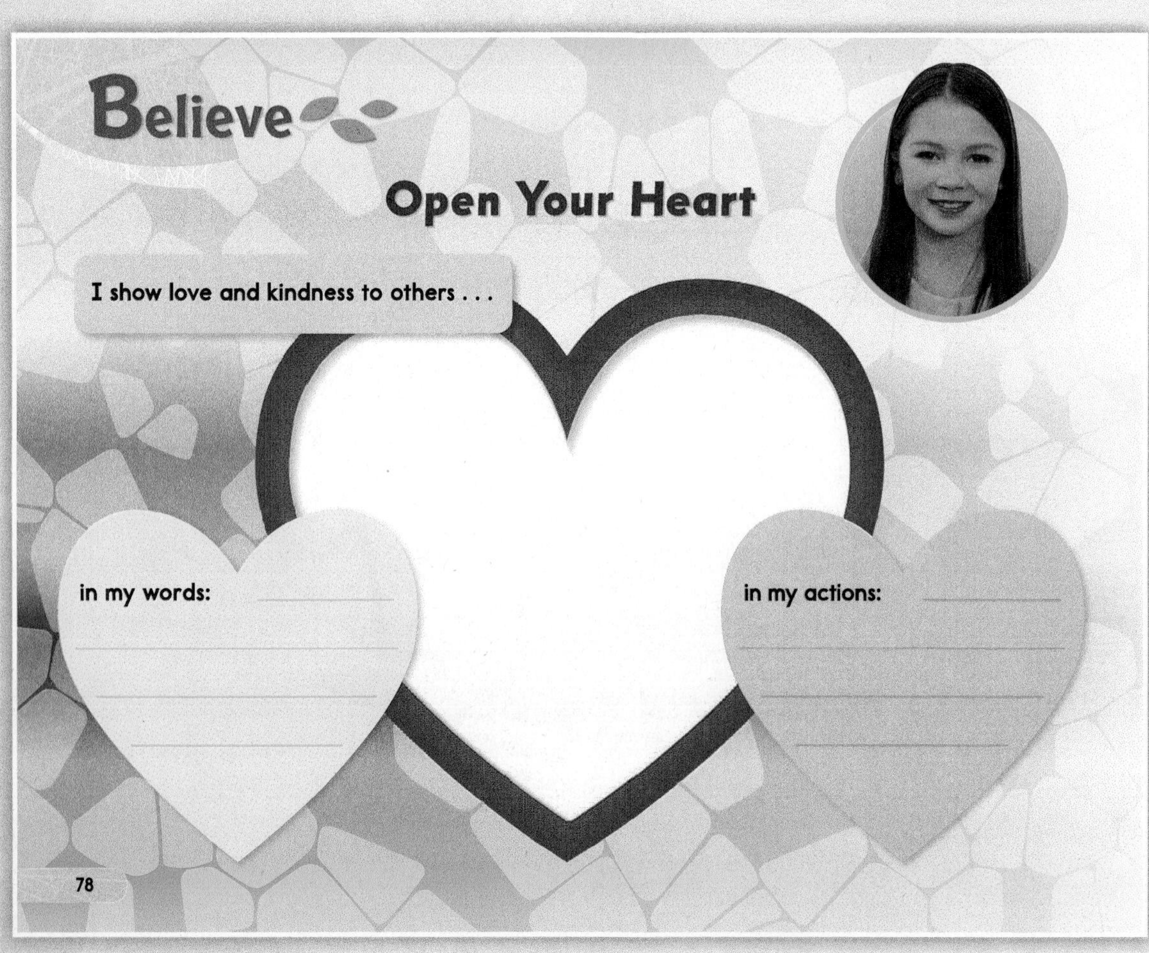
Believe
Open Your Heart
I show love and kindness to others . . .
in my words:
in my actions:
78

Caring and Helping

Introduce this page by saying, "Each time we say or do something kind, we show others the love of God."

Read aloud the first paragraph.

Ask *In what ways can you help others in need?*

Read the second paragraph.

Ask *In what ways did Jesus help people in need?* Emphasize that followers of Jesus love and care for others.

Read the Scripture quote from John's Gospel together. Ask the children for examples of ways God loves us. Invite the children to close their eyes and silently answer this question: *What are some ways I can follow Jesus' example of love?*

Activity

- Explain that God has given each of us special gifts and talents to be used to help others.
- Distribute drawing paper, colored pencils or crayons, and a large unlined index card.
- Invite the children to write their name in the center of their index card. Have them write words or draw pictures around their name of their different gifts and talents. You may wish to provide examples such as cooking, drawing, and the ability to read or act out stories in an entertaining way.

Notes ____________________

Caring and Helping

Each of us needs the help and care of others. We may need care because we are sick. Maybe we need help with chores or homework. Sometimes we just need someone to show us love and care because we are feeling sad. In the same way, sometimes others need our help and care.

In what ways can I help others in need?

Jesus showed love and care for all people. He comforted and healed those who were sick. He spent time with those who were lonely or rejected. He was patient and forgiving. Jesus calls us to do as he did and help and care for others.

"Love one another as I love you."

JOHN 15:12

Believe

The Word of the Lord

Share that Jesus cared very much for his disciples. In the three years he spent with them, he helped them to become a community of people who loved and cared for one another and for people in need outside their community.

Read aloud the introductory paragraph before the Scripture.

Explain that the children are going to hear a reading from the Bible, the living Word of God. This is a reading from the Gospel of Matthew.

Guide the children through an adaptation of *Lectio Divina*, a special way to pray with Scripture. Quiet the children, and ask them to listen carefully to the Scripture reading as you read it aloud.

Reflect on the reading by inviting the children to:

- Take a moment to think about what they heard.
- Silently answer the following questions for reflection (be sure to pause after each question): *What word or words did you hear? What do you think Jesus is saying to you?*
- Quietly hold these words in their hearts. (Pause in prayer.)
- Share aloud in one or two words what they heard. Describe what they were feeling in their hearts. (Accept all responses.)

Guide the children through an adaption of *Visio Divina*, a special way to pray with Scripture art. Quiet the children, and invite them to take their time looking at the illustration on pages 80 and 81. Read aloud the Scripture once again. Invite the children to silently answer these questions: *What do you see? What does it mean to you? What do you imagine Jesus inviting you to see? What do you think this means for you?*

The Word of the Lord

After Jesus had risen from the dead, eleven of his disciples gathered on a mountain in Galilee. Jesus had told them to meet him there.

Based on MATTHEW 28:16–20

When the disciples saw the Risen Christ appear, they could hardly believe their eyes. They worshiped him. Jesus said to them, "All power in heaven and on earth has been given to me. Go, therefore, and make disciples of all nations, baptizing them in the name of the Father, and of the Son, and of the holy Spirit" (Matthew 28:18–19).

Jesus wanted his disciples to share God's love with all people. Jesus wanted his disciples to teach others how to be his followers and friends. Jesus promised his disciples that he would always be with them. He said, "I am with you always" (Matthew 28:20).

80

Share After the silent reflection, allow time for sharing aloud responses to these questions. Then invite the children to look again at the picture and silently answer the questions: *What are some things this picture tells you about the Risen Jesus' message to his disciples? What does it tell you about how the disciples feel about the message? How?* Invite volunteers to share their responses aloud.

Check comprehension by asking the following questions:

Why did Jesus gather his disciples on a mountaintop? (Jesus wanted to give them an important message.)

In whose name were the disciples to baptize new members of their community? (They were to baptize in the name of the Father, and of the Son, and of the Holy Spirit.)

What did Jesus promise his disciples? (He promised to be with them always.)

Scripture Background

The Risen Jesus appeared to his disciples immediately before his Ascension, his return to his Father in heaven. Jesus told his disciples to come to a certain mountain in the region called Galilee. The disciples had been staying in Jerusalem and had to travel a long distance to get to the mountain. Jesus presented them with an important mission: The disciples were to help others come to know Jesus Christ and his saving truth. Jesus let them know that they should not be afraid or lose courage. He would send the Holy Spirit to guide them in their mission. Jesus kept his promise when he sent the Holy Spirit to his disciples at Pentecost.

Notes ______________________________

____

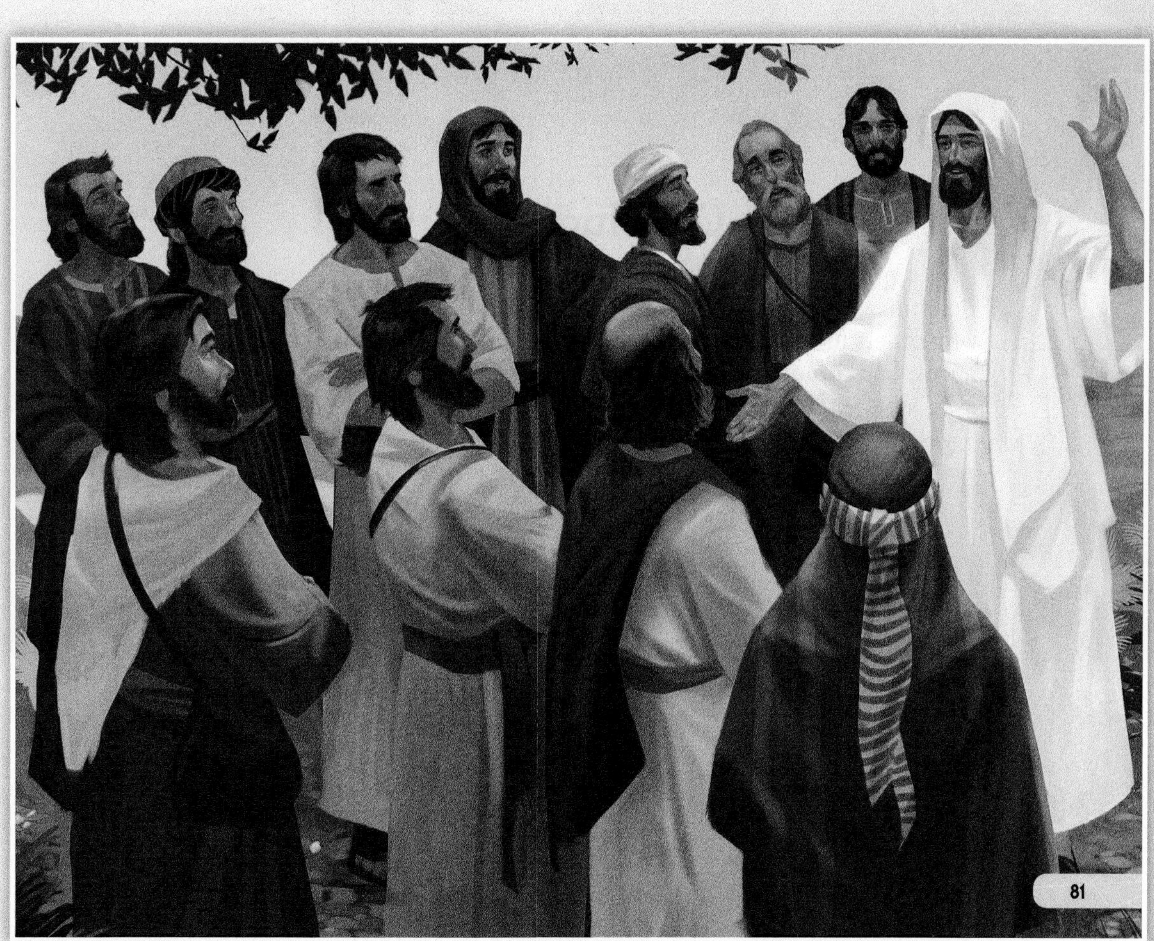

Celebrate

Concluding Rites

Guide the children to recall the command Jesus gave to his disciples before his return to his Father in heaven.

Read aloud the text on page 82.

Ask *With what does the celebration of Mass end?* (The Mass ends with the Concluding Rites.) *What does the priest give to us during the Concluding Rites?* (The priest gives a blessing to us, asking God to keep us in his care.) *What word do we use to respond to the blessing?* ("Amen")

Direct attention to the photograph on this page showing a priest giving the final blessing. Explain, "Sometimes when people are getting ready to go on a journey, they receive a blessing before they leave. This is what happens at the end of Mass. We get ready to begin our journey, our daily lives, as disciples of Jesus. Before we leave, we receive God's blessing."

Encourage the children to listen closely at Mass each Sunday to remember which dismissal the priest or deacon uses. Point out that we are sent out at the end of Mass to continue the work of Jesus. And Jesus is with us, too, as he promised.

Celebrating Cultural Diversity

Traditions and customs from cultures that make up our one Church

Catholics in the Philippines have a Lenten custom, *Visita Iglesia*, of visting seven churches on Holy Thursday. They often begin their church visits after celebrating Mass, reflecting on the Last Supper, and praying before the Blessed Sacrament. Friends and families travel to other churches that they have selected. If the churches are in close proximity they may choose to walk. Whether they travel by foot or by car, this custom helps those on the "journey" to remember their Catholic identity. The church visits are usually completed by midnight in order to prepare for Good Friday.

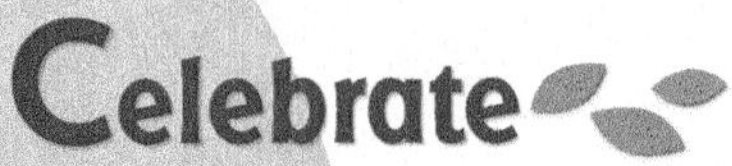

Concluding Rites

Jesus sent his disciples out to continue his work. We are disciples of Jesus. He wants us to keep doing his work, too. He wants us to share God's love with others in our homes, schools, parishes, neighborhoods, cities or towns, and throughout the world. God's grace helps us to do all that he asks. We are reminded of this call at Mass.

The celebration of the Mass ends with the **Concluding Rites**, which include a greeting and blessing, dismissal, and reverence of the altar. At the end of Mass, together with the priest, we ask the Lord to be with us. Then the priest gives us a blessing. This final **blessing** is a prayer asking God to keep us in his care. The priest blesses us with the Sign of the Cross as he says,

"May almighty God bless you,
the Father, and the Son, † and the Holy Spirit."

We respond, "Amen."

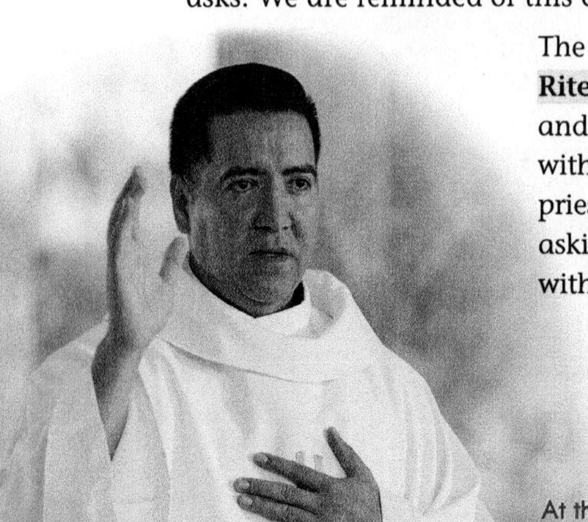

At the end of Mass, we make the Sign of the Cross as the priest blesses us in God's name.

82

Read aloud the text on page 83. Then practice the final response by saying, "Go in peace." Invite the response, "Thanks be to God."

Direct attention to the illustration showing a parish community after Sunday Mass. Point out that the people are being friendly. Ask: *What do you think the people are talking about?* Together, make up a story about what some of the people in the picture may be saying, or describe what you talk about after Mass.

Explain that the people in the illustration are baptized members of the Catholic Church. Ask: *What mission do they all share?*

CATHOLIC IDENTITY

Read aloud the statement. Pray together: *Dear God, we are thankful for your love and care. Help us to love you with all our hearts and to share your love with others.*

Activity

- Invite the children to think about the descriptions they gave of their gifts and talents. Explain that each member of their family also has special gifts from God. A family can work together to serve others.
- Have the children name one way their family helps others.

Words of Faith

Concluding Rites (page 82)

blessing (page 82)

Notes ______________________

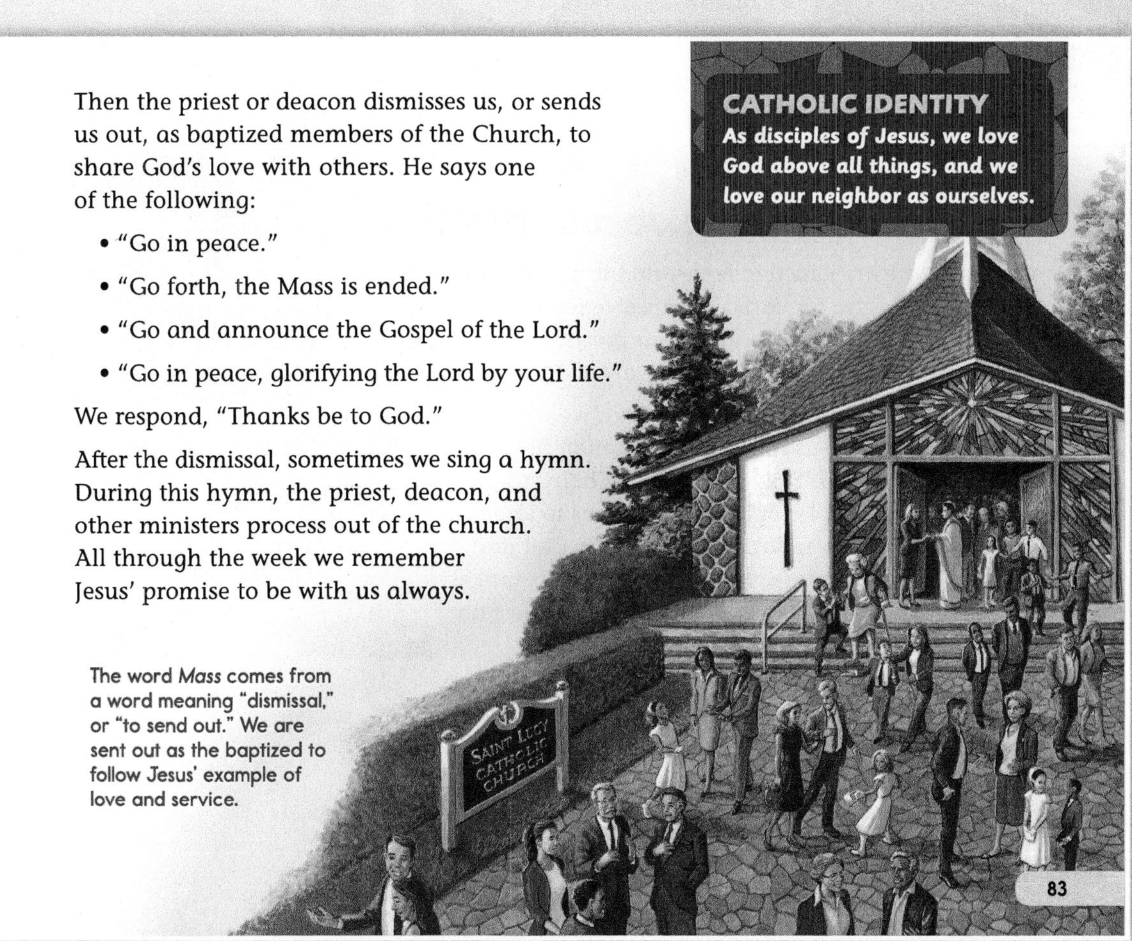

CATHOLIC IDENTITY
As disciples of Jesus, we love God above all things, and we love our neighbor as ourselves.

Then the priest or deacon dismisses us, or sends us out, as baptized members of the Church, to share God's love with others. He says one of the following:

- "Go in peace."
- "Go forth, the Mass is ended."
- "Go and announce the Gospel of the Lord."
- "Go in peace, glorifying the Lord by your life."

We respond, "Thanks be to God."

After the dismissal, sometimes we sing a hymn. During this hymn, the priest, deacon, and other ministers process out of the church. All through the week we remember Jesus' promise to be with us always.

The word *Mass* comes from a word meaning "dismissal," or "to send out." We are sent out as the baptized to follow Jesus' example of love and service.

83

Celebrate

Continuing Jesus' Work

Read page 84. Stress that each time we receive Jesus in Holy Communion our friendship with Jesus grows.

Ask *How does receiving Jesus in Holy Communion help us?* (Receiving Holy Communion helps us to love God and others. The Eucharist helps us to become stronger disciples of Jesus, and helps us to join our parish community in loving and serving God and others.) Emphasize the importance of receiving Holy Communion whenever we participate in the celebration of the Eucharist and are in a state of grace. Turn to page 92 and talk about "Leading a Sacramental Life." We are joined even more closely to Christ, which strengthens the unity of the whole Church as the Mystical Body of Christ.

Read the text on page 85. Point out that these are just a few ways in which we can love and serve God and others. Add your own ways to the list. Together, act out people loving and serving God in some of these ways.

Catholic Faith and Life

Direct attention to the feature on the Most Blessed Sacrament on page 85. Look at the "Parish Church Tour" on pages 4 and 5 of this book. Point out the tabernacle. Also point out the sanctuary lamp. Explain that the lamp remains lit to remind us that Jesus is present in the Most Blessed Sacrament. *Tabernacle* and *Most Blessed Sacrament* are also defined in the Glossary. Turn to page 94 and share a "Prayer to Jesus before the Most Blessed Sacrament." Encourage the children to visit Jesus in the Most Blessed Sacrament and spend time with him in prayer.

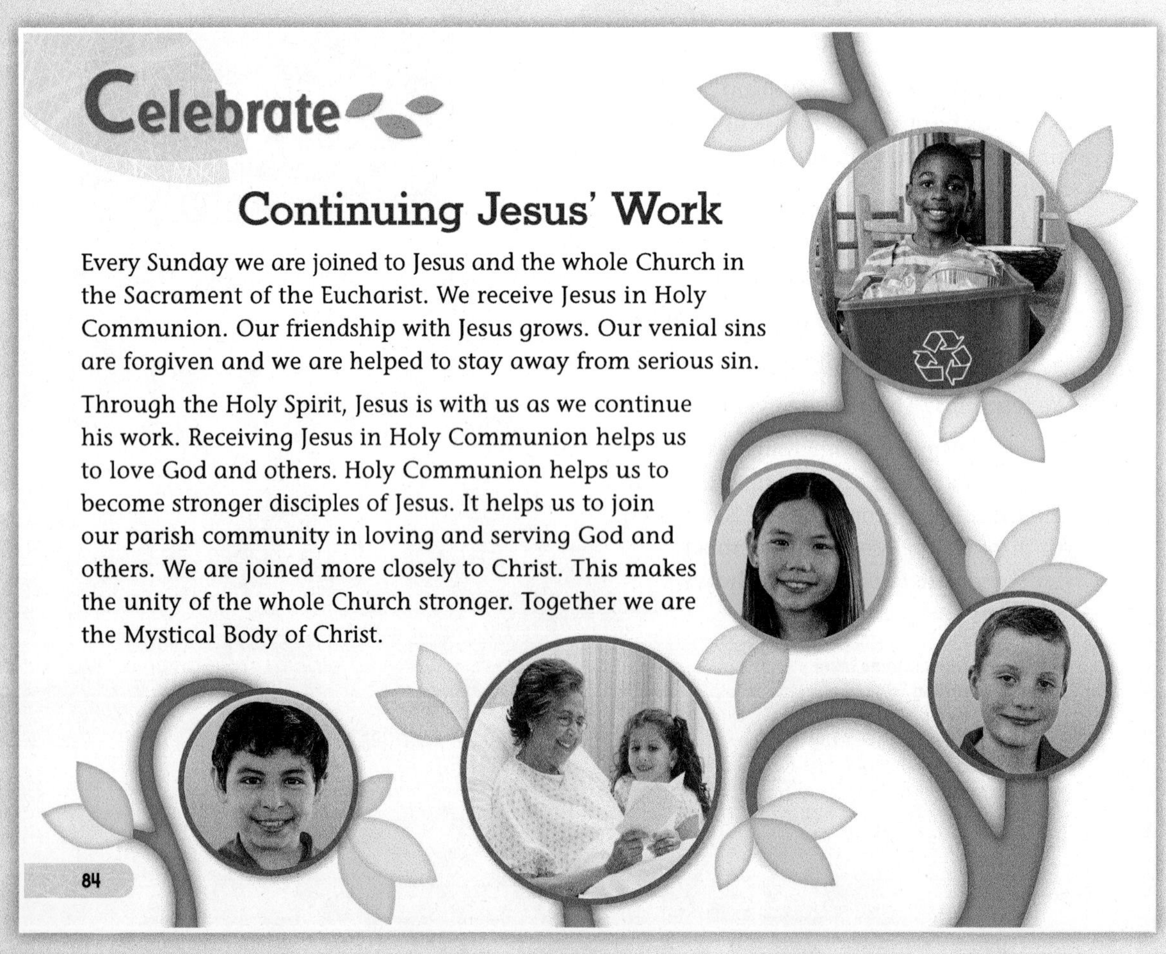
Celebrate

Continuing Jesus' Work

Every Sunday we are joined to Jesus and the whole Church in the Sacrament of the Eucharist. We receive Jesus in Holy Communion. Our friendship with Jesus grows. Our venial sins are forgiven and we are helped to stay away from serious sin.

Through the Holy Spirit, Jesus is with us as we continue his work. Receiving Jesus in Holy Communion helps us to love God and others. Holy Communion helps us to become stronger disciples of Jesus. It helps us to join our parish community in loving and serving God and others. We are joined more closely to Christ. This makes the unity of the whole Church stronger. Together we are the Mystical Body of Christ.

84

Note: After the children have received their First Holy Communion, ask the following questions to help them remember the time of preparation, their First Communion experience, and the deeper meaning of the celebration of the Sacrament of the Eucharist for them now.

Since your Baptism, who has helped you to grow closer to Jesus?
Who in your family helped you prepare for the celebration of your First Holy Communion?
Who celebrated the Sacrament of the Eucharist with you?
What made receiving Jesus in Holy Communion special for you?
What did you hear in the songs, prayers, and readings of the celebration?
How can you make Jesus part of your life each Sunday?
How can your family help?
How can you share Jesus with others all through the week?

Activity

- Explain that the Sacrament of the Eucharist and receiving Jesus in Holy Communion helps us to understand Jesus' love and how we are to love others.
- Together, reread the list of ways to love and serve God and others on page 85.
- Encourage the children to choose one way they can serve others.

Notes

As disciples of Jesus Christ we can love and serve God and others in many ways. Here are a few of those ways.

- Help out at home or in school.
- Do something kind for a friend or neighbor.
- Give to a food or clothing drive.
- Send a get-well card or make a visit to someone who is sick.
- Pray for others, and especially people who are poor or hungry.
- Forgive others or ask for their forgiveness.

At Mass, after Holy Communion, there may be consecrated Hosts that have not been received. These Hosts are placed in reserve in the *tabernacle* to bring to the sick and for the adoration of the faithful. The *Most Blessed Sacrament* is another name for the Eucharist. We can visit the church and pray to Jesus, who is present in the Most Blessed Sacrament. We can ask Jesus to help us love and care for others.

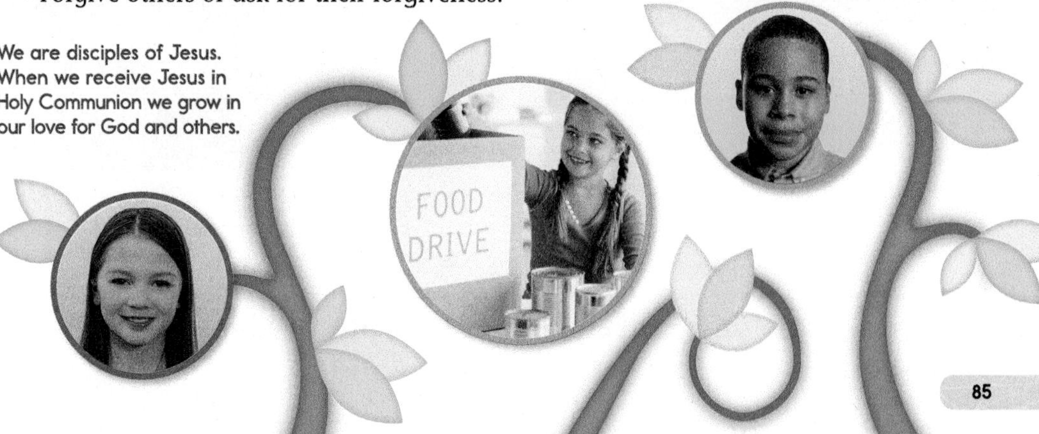

We are disciples of Jesus. When we receive Jesus in Holy Communion we grow in our love for God and others.

85

Live

Become What You Believe

Explain that we can love and serve God and others in many places—at home, at school, at church, and in any place where we meet other people. We can also be caring and generous with people who may live far away from us.

Direct attention to the statement in bold at the bottom of the page. Ask the group to read it aloud together and think about what it means in their lives.

Activity

- Read aloud the sentence starter on page 86. Distribute colored pencils or crayons. Invite the children to draw themselves responding to Jesus' call. To help them get started you may wish to say the following: *God calls each one of us to be kind and loving toward others. Think about times when you saw someone who needed your help. What did you do to help them?*
- Encourage the children to share their pictures with the group.

Notes ______________________________

____

____

____

____

Live

Become What You Believe

Complete the statement by drawing yourself in the scene.

Jesus calls me, and I respond by . . .

As a disciple I am sent out to love and serve God and others.

Discipleship in Action

Explain that the saint the children will hear about, Saint Pedro Calungsod, enjoyed learning about God. He also helped others come to know and believe in God.

Read aloud the story of Saint Pedro Calungsod.

Share key points from the story. Talk about how Saint Pedro Calungsod helped others become followers of Jesus.

Explain that we can all share what we know and believe as disciples of Jesus.

Notes ______________________

____

____

____

Activity

- Have the children complete the sentence starter. Encourage them to share their responses.
- Have the children make a poster they could use to teach others about Jesus.
- Distribute colored pencils and drawing paper.
- Write the following heading on the board for the children to copy: "All About Jesus"
- After the children have finished copying, have them write and draw pictures that can help others know more about Jesus.
- Invite the children to share their work with the group.

Discipleship in Action

Saint Pedro Calungsod (1654–1672)

Pedro Calungsod grew up in the Philippines in the 1600s. Pedro learned the Catholic faith at school and was a faithful Christian as a child. By the time he was a teenager Pedro was already a catechist. A catechist is a person who teaches others about God and how to live as Jesus did. When Pedro was fourteen, he became a missionary in Guam, an island where people did not know about God. There he spread the Good News of Jesus' love for all people. Through Pedro's teaching and example, many people became followers of Jesus and were baptized.

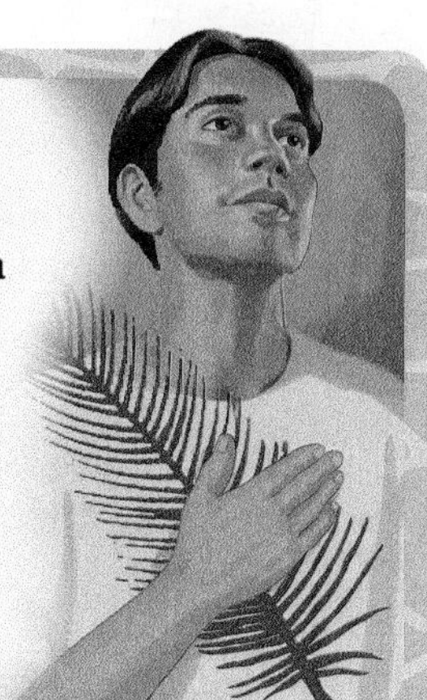

I can help others know about Jesus' love by . . .

____

____

____

Living as the Body of Christ

Live

We Are the Body of Christ/ *Somos el Cuerpo de Cristo*

Read and familiarize yourself with the prayer and the music selection. To prepare the environment, arrange the following items on a small table:

- white tablecloth
- glass bowl half full of holy water
- baptismal candle in holder near bowl
- Bible on a table stand

You will also need:

- CD player
- Music CD queued to play track "We Are the Body of Christ/*Somos el Cuerpo de Cristo*"

Invite the children to gather around the table with their books. Teach them song "We Are the Body of Christ/*Somos el Cuerpo de Cristo.*" Ask the children to quiet themselves for prayer. Briefly describe the ritual actions in the prayer—blessing with holy water and sharing a sign of peace. Remind the children to follow your lead when you go to bless yourself with holy water. Pray the prayer together, ending with the Lord's Prayer (page 93 of child's book).

Conclude the prayer ritual with the following "mystagogy," or reflection on the experience. Invite the children to give one- or two-word responses to the following:

- *How did it feel to bless your head, your lips, and your heart?*
- *What words from the song do you remember most?*
- *What does it mean to you to be part of the Body of Christ?*

Live

We Are the Body of Christ/ *Somos el Cuerpo de Cristo*

Leader: Let us make the Sign of the Cross and then sing together.

All: (*Refrain*) *Somos el cuerpo de Cristo.* We are the body of Christ.

Hemos oído el llamado; we've answered "Yes" to the call of the Lord.

Somos el cuerpo de Cristo. We are the body of Christ.

Traemos su santo mensaje. We come to bring the good news to the world.

(*After each verse, sing:* We are the body of Christ.)

Bringing the light of God's mercy to others (*Sing*)

Serving each other we build up the kingdom. (*Sing*)

All are invited to feast in the banquet. (*Sing*)

(*Sing refrain.*)

Leader: Christ lives in our thoughts, words, and actions, so come forward now to make the Sign of the Cross on your forehead, lips, and heart with the holy water.

All: (*Sing refrain.*)

Leader: Let us offer a sign of peace and pray as Jesus taught us.

All: Our Father . . .

Living Faith at Home

Encourage family participation by having the children take home the double-sided "Living Faith at Home" page.

Living Faith at Home

Jesus said, "I am with you always."

MATTHEW 28:20

Take a few minutes to reflect on the Scripture art. Ask God to open your eyes and your heart. What feelings are you experiencing? What do you think it was like to hear Jesus speak in person? What is Jesus saying to you right now? Pray a silent prayer of gratitude.

89

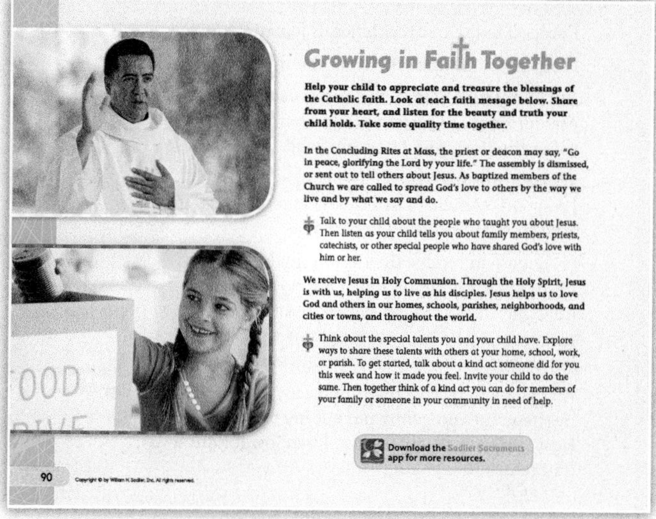

Growing in Faith Together

Help your child to appreciate and treasure the blessings of the Catholic faith. Look at each faith message below. Share from your heart, and listen for the beauty and truth your child holds. Take some quality time together.

In the Concluding Rites at Mass, the priest or deacon may say, "Go in peace, glorifying the Lord by your life." The assembly is dismissed, or sent out to tell others about Jesus. As baptized members of the Church we are called to spread God's love to others by the way we live and by what we say and do.

Talk to your child about the people who taught you about Jesus. Then listen as your child tells you about family members, priests, catechists, or other special people who have shared God's love with him or her.

We receive Jesus in Holy Communion. Through the Holy Spirit, Jesus is with us, helping us to live as his disciples. Jesus helps us to love God and others in our homes, schools, parishes, neighborhoods, and cities or towns, and throughout the world.

Think about the special talents you and your child have. Explore ways to share these talents with others at your home, school, work, or parish. To get started, talk about a kind act someone did for you this week and how it made you feel. Invite your child to do the same. Then together think of a kind act you can do for members of your family or someone in your community in need of help.

Download the Sadlier Sacraments app for more resources.

90

Celebrating Inclusion

Strategies and tips for including children with disabilities

Use the following tips to teach this chapter through a multisensory approach, which may benefit not only children with learning differences but others as well. The more we teach in a multisensory approach that includes auditory, visual, and tactile-kinesthetic (hands-on) opportunities for learning, the more learners we will reach when we teach.

Believe On page 79, have children with language difficulties work with partners to locate pictures in their book or from magazine pictures (pre-selected so they don't see inappropriate images) that depict people helping others.

For page 80, write the phrase *Jesus said, "I am with you always."* on the board. Visual or hands-on learners will benefit from working with a partner to use alphabet magnets or letter titles from a word-related board game to compose what Jesus said.

Celebrate Tactile-kinesthetic learners will especially benefit from practicing the four forms of dismissal on page 82 as follows: Organize the children into four groups, assign each group one of the dismissal forms, and have them make a poster showing the words to the dismissal along with artwork that depicts the message. As each group proclaims its assigned dismissal, have the entire class respond, "Thanks be to God." Extend the activity by role-playing the parts of priest, deacon, and assembly.

On page 85, visual and hands-on learners will benefit from seeing photos of tabernacles. Point out that every tabernacle looks different. Tactile-kinesthetic and visual learners will benefit from seeing the tabernacle in the parish church. Take time to pray individually, or as a group, while visiting the Blessed Sacrament.

Live On pages 86 and 87, allow children who have difficulty with fine motor skills or visual impairments to respond verbally.

On page 88, provide instruments for hands-on learners to use while singing. During the final blessing and the sign of peace be sensitive to children who are uncomfortable with touch.

Notes ______________________

____

How to Receive Jesus in Holy Communion

How to Receive Jesus in Holy Communion

When I receive the Body of Christ in Holy Communion, this is what I do:

I bow my head.

I receive the Host in my hand.

I receive the Host on my tongue.

I process to the altar with hands joined in prayer.

I sing the communion hymn or chant with the assembly.

When my turn comes, the priest, deacon, or extraordinary minister of Holy Communion raises the Host, and I bow my head.

When I hear the words, "The Body of Christ," I respond, "Amen." I can choose to receive the Host in my hand or on my tongue.

If I choose to receive the Host in my hand, I place my left hand on top of my right hand (or the opposite if I am left-handed). After the Host is placed in my hand, I eat it right away, fold my hands in prayer, and return to my seat.

If I choose to receive the Host on my tongue, I hold my head up and gently put out my tongue. After the Host is placed on my tongue, I swallow it right away, and return to my seat.

91

If I am going to receive from the chalice, I first swallow the Host. I walk to the priest, deacon, or extraordinary minister of Holy Communion holding the chalice.

I receive from the chalice.

The chalice is raised before me, and I bow my head.

When I hear the words "The Blood of Christ," I respond, "Amen." Then I take a sip from the chalice. After I receive from the chalice, I fold my hands in prayer and return to my seat.

After I receive Communion, this is what I do:

I sing the Communion chant, or song, with my parish family.

Once the chant or song is completed, I spend time in quiet prayer.

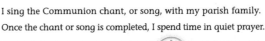

Eucharistic Fast

As a sign of respect and reverence for Jesus in the Eucharist, we must have not taken any food or drink for one hour before receiving Holy Communion. This is called the Eucharistic fast. Water and medicine may be taken during the Eucharistic fast.

Leading a Sacramental Life

Receive Holy Communion often and the Sacrament of Penance and Reconciliation regularly. Follow the laws of the Church, which say: We must attend Mass on Sundays and other Holy Days of Obligation. We must receive Holy Communion once a year, at least during the Easter season. We must confess our sins once a year if we have committed mortal, or serious, sin.

When we receive Holy Communion, we must always be in the state of grace. Anyone who has committed a mortal sin must receive absolution in the Sacrament of Penance and Reconciliation before receiving Holy Communion.

92

- Read aloud the steps for receiving the Body of Christ in Holy Communion.
- Review each part of the process, and review with the children the meaning of any Words of Faith.
- Remind the children that they may choose to receive the Host in their hand or on their tongue.
- Read aloud the steps for receiving from the chalice.
- Remind the children that when the Host or chalice is raised, they bow their head as a sign of reverence.
- Practice together their "Amen" response when they hear the words "The Body of Christ" or "The Blood of Christ."
- You may wish to review with the children the "Prayer before Communion" and the "Prayer after Communion" on page 94.

Lord's Prayer

Our Father, who art in heaven,
hallowed be thy name;
thy kingdom come;
thy will be done on earth
as it is in heaven.
Give us this day our daily bread;
and forgive us our trespasses
as we forgive those
who trespass against us;
and lead us not into temptation,
but deliver us from evil.
Amen.

Apostles' Creed

I believe in God, the Father almighty,
Creator of heaven and earth,
and in Jesus Christ, his only Son, our Lord,
who was conceived by the Holy Spirit,
born of the Virgin Mary,
suffered under Pontius Pilate,
was crucified, died and was buried;
he descended into hell;
on the third day he rose again from
the dead;
he ascended into heaven,
and is seated at the right hand
of God the Father almighty;
from there he will come to judge
the living and the dead.

I believe in the Holy Spirit,
the holy catholic Church,
the communion of saints,
the forgiveness of sins,
the resurrection of the body,
and life everlasting.
Amen.

Prayer before Communion

Jesus, you are the Bread of Life.
Thank you for sharing your life with me.
Help me always to be your friend
and disciple.

Jesus, help me to welcome you into
my heart.
Help me to be true to you always.

Prayer after Communion

Jesus, you do such great things for me!
You fill me with your life.
Help me to grow in loving you and
others.

Jesus, thank you for coming to me in
Holy Communion.
I love you very much. You come to live
within me.
You fill me with your life.
Help me to be and do all that you wish.

Prayer before the Most Blessed Sacrament

Jesus,
you are God-with-us,
especially in this Sacrament of
the Eucharist.
You love me as I am and help me grow.

Come and be with me
in all my joys and sorrows.
Help me share your peace and love
with everyone I meet.
I ask in your name.
Amen.

GLOSSARY

actual grace (page 14) grace at work in our daily lives, helping us to do good

altar (page 54) the special table that is the center of the celebration of the Liturgy of the Eucharist, also called the Table of the Lord

ambo (page 43) a sacred reading stand called the Table of the Word of God. The ambo is used for the proclamation of Scripture in the liturgy.

assembly (page 26) the community of people who join together for the celebration of the Eucharist or other sacraments

Blessed Trinity (page 12) the Three Persons in One God: God the Father, God the Son, and God the Holy Spirit

blessing (page 82) the prayer that the priest prays over the assembly at the end of Mass, blessing us with the Sign of the Cross and asking God to keep us in his care

Book of the Gospels (page 43) a special book that contains the Gospels of Matthew, Mark, Luke, and John

chalice (page 57) the special cup into which the priest pours the grape wine that becomes the Blood of Christ during the Liturgy of the Eucharist

Church (page 12) the community of people who are baptized and are called to follow Jesus Christ

Concluding Rites (page 82) the last part of the Mass, which includes a greeting and blessing, dismissal, and reverence of the altar

Consecration (page 56) the part of the Eucharistic Prayer when, by the power of the Holy Spirit and through the words and actions of the priest, the bread and wine become the Body and Blood of Christ

Creed (page 42) the prayer in which we proclaim the faith of the Church

Eucharistic Prayer (page 56) the center of the Mass and the Church's greatest prayer of praise and thanksgiving

Gospel (page 41) the Good News about Jesus Christ and how to live as his disciples. The Gospels are four books of the New Testament that tell about Jesus' life and teachings.

Holy Communion (page 68) the receiving of the bread and wine that have become the Body and Blood of Christ at Mass

homily (page 42) the talk given by the priest or deacon at Mass that helps us understand the readings

Host (page 69) the Bread that has become the Body of Christ

Introductory Rites (page 28) the first part of the Mass; prayers and actions that prepare us to listen to the Word of God and celebrate the Eucharist

GLOSSARY

Last Supper (page 52) the last meal Jesus shared with his disciples, on the night before he died

Lectionary (page 43) a special book from which the first two readings of the Mass are read

lector (page 43) a reader who reads the Scripture readings at Mass except for the Gospel

Liturgy of the Eucharist (page 54) the part of the Mass in which the bread and wine become the Body and Blood of Jesus Christ

Liturgy of the Word (page 40) the part of the Mass in which we listen to God's Word being proclaimed

Lord's Day (page 27) Sunday is called the Lord's Day. Its celebration is from Saturday evening through Sunday until midnight.

Mass (page 13) the celebration of the Eucharist

Most Blessed Sacrament (page 85) another name for the Eucharist, the consecrated Hosts

paten (page 57) the special plate on which the priest places the wheat bread that becomes the Body of Christ during the Liturgy of the Eucharist

Prayer of the Faithful (page 43) the prayer after the Creed during the Liturgy of the Word in which we pray for the needs of all God's people

psalm (page 41) a song of praise from the Old Testament

Real Presence (page 57) Jesus Christ being truly present in the Eucharist

sacraments (page 14) special signs given to us by Jesus through which we share in God's life and love

sacrifice (page 55) an offering of a gift to God

sanctifying grace (page 14) the gift of grace that we receive in the sacraments that helps us to respond to God's love and live as Jesus did

sign of peace (page 69) at Mass, a sign that we share with the people who are near us to show that we are united to Christ and to one another

tabernacle (page 85) the special place in the church in which the Most Blessed Sacrament is placed in reserve

vestments (page 26) the special clothing that priests and deacons wear to celebrate Mass or other rites

worship (page 26) to give God thanks and praise